The Petals
of
Nora Rose

A Reflective
Compilation of Essays

TAMRA SEASE

ISBN: 1500570966
ISBN 13: 9781500570965

To my Heavenly Father for being the God of the universe and still having time to lean Your ear towards my heart; for seeing my core, for unworthy grace and undeserving mercy; for knowing my truth and unfathomably loving me the same; for allowing Your Son to take the heat for my disgracefulness and daily renewing my faith with fresh discoveries of who You are…I thank You.

To Daddy for wisdom and the patience to pick me up after every fall

To Mommy for strength and the boldness to confront everything with optimism

To Jacque for your gentle spirit and endless laughter

To Brandon for adventure and creativity

To Jean Box for coloring my world with a love that makes the heart of God smile

To Pastor & First Lady Trina for instruction and the courage to dream beyond, beyond

To the First Baptist Church of Glenarden for faithfully developing an imperfect disciple

To Hampton University for the standard of excellence

To my Godparents, Inner Circle, and extended family for accountability and inspiration

To Jason T. for the push, the prayers, and the perspective

To Aunt Carolyn for giving an effective and faithful word in due season

To Ceron for catching every tear and showing the beauty in every storm

To Crystal J. for being my vault and cherishing the core of who God created me to be

To Richard for the significance of closed doors… I get it now.

To Jared for your epic brilliance and admirable integrity

To Melvin for being my starship and seeing through every false façade

To Josh for every challenge, every dance, and every platform

To Tony for transparency, trustworthiness, and infinite encouragement

To Jere' for discerning my confusion and prayers that move mountains

To Karmia for perseverance; history will forever treasure your footprints in its sand.

To Nakeisha for escaping comfort zones and breaking free from conformity

To Endia for untangling so many fears and your boldness to breathe

To LaTrisha for understanding the highs and lows of my heart

To AJB for reminding me, regardless of my past, God can still use someone like me

To April for correction covered in compassion and remaining a voice of reason

To Teresa H. for exceptional guidance and incomparable character... you empower me.

To Miles for the never-ending journey... I wouldn't trade our story for anything.

To Collins for setting tones of artistic liberty and faithfully remaining in my corner

To Aaron for discipline, keeping me focused, and literally changing my life

To LaNyce for being a wellspring of innovated vision... I cherish your intellect.

To Riche, Jade, and Loleta for exemplifying the art of being a lady in waiting

To Dee, Melinda, Sherese, Melanie, and George for your time and ingenuity.

To Monique, Monae, Tinesha, Ericaa & Lilybelle for fervent passion and ambition

To my beautiful cluster of nieces, nephews, and Camden for purpose

To Rodney, Tosin, Tanesia, Charcelle, Nicky, and Dawn...I'm sorry for letting you down.

To Yusuf... VIRESCIT VULNERE VIRTUS. *Rest peacefully my brother.*

And to Nana for the example...

This is for you.

Table of Contents

Preface

Not a day goes by that I don't think of my grandmother. She was the epitome of grace, humility, and wisdom. She lived a life that showered her friends and family with guidance and truth. Her strength surpassed my logic and the reach of her compassion continues to remain unfathomable. I think of her in the most surreal moments of any day. Whether enchanted by burnt-orange evening moons or breathtaking lavender horizons, I dream of her. And in those moments where my mind finds no end, I live with one regret...I didn't appreciate her enough while she was here.

This book is my tribute to Eleanor Jewett Sease. My Nana. My Nora Rose.

Few know that my passion for writing was birthed from midday homework sessions under her supervision. She was a renowned teacher within our family, having educated a plethora of her own siblings, including my own. She would spend endless and meticulous time ensuring our assignments were neat, completed, and exceptional. One of my most memorable moments with her was shared in my senior year of high school. Consumed with the highs and lows of my adolescence, I was unmotivated to write my final AP English essay. Sitting at her kitchen counter as she prepared dinner, I couldn't wrap my mind around the point of transparently writing this particular assignment because I was convinced that no one cared. There was no way humanly possible that anyone would be enthused or changed by what I had to share. Needless to say, I was over it.

As I pouted, Nana continued to fry fish, peel potatoes, and shuck corn. She wasn't moved with the challenge set before me nor phased by my dramatics. After providing a complex illustration, she began to ask a series of questions, not only to motivate my thinking but also to develop a plan of action to fulfill the task in front of me. Each question forced me to step outside of my comfort zone and do something I didn't feel like doing – reflect. She forced me to turn the light on myself and see the death in my perception. Our conversation closed with a notion that I remember vividly to this day: *"Writers have an obligation to write what others can't say. Their words bring life to dead situations. It's time to help someone live."*

Nana went to be with the Lord in May 2005. I believe that when she passed, my voice changed. My perspective changed. Life changed. As I grew older and lived a little longer, the world began to throw unexpected twists and turns. Yet, every time a spirit of frustration would surface, so would flashes of that AP English afternoon. My mind would immediately revert back to that kitchen counter and into a subconscious period of self-reflection. I would be lying if I said that every reflection resulted in wise decision-making or that I learned each lesson once and then progressed to the next. That, I promise you, is everything that didn't occur. Pride, arrogance, and flat-out stupidity were the cause of many situations resulting in nose-dive pools of failure. Yet, through it all, God whispered His truth, many through the conduit memories of my grandmother.

One of Nana's most prized possessions was a rose garden that aligned the right side of her driveway. She nurtured her roses as she did with her family – time and tenderness. Often times, in the midst of tending to these earthly jewels, petals would fall from their *corolla*. The corolla is the colorful collection of petals that bloom from a flower. Ironically, no matter how much the corolla desires to bloom, its blossoming is contingent upon the cultivation of the plant. If the plant isn't tilled and groomed responsibly and consistently, the plant will die and so will its ability to reproduce.

This book holds a series of monumental petals that bloomed from the life of my grandmother. Some she shared. Others she inspired.

This collection of essays evolved from scars that silence wouldn't heal. My disguises grew old and the efforts of trying to keep it together became exhausting. I decided to take my past out of the closet, dust off the shame and embarrassment of its contents, and made myself a mandated priority. Just like Nana, I began to ask myself a series of questions and dared to be honest with the woman in the mirror.

This by no means is a culmination of advice that I've mastered; I'm still living and learning, but this time everyday is more purposeful. I pray each petal touches your heart, each reflection challenges intense periods of transformation, and each found truth evokes a passion in you to help someone else live the way Nana would want us to.

With infinite love,

TAM

Silently a flower blooms, in silence it falls away;
yet here, now, at this moment, at this place,
the world of the flower, the whole of the world is blooming.
This is the talk of the flower, the truth of the blossom:
The glory of eternal life is fully shining here.

ZENKEI SHIBAYAMA

PETAL I
The Little Things

In the fall of 2011, my beautiful niece Payton saw rain for the very first time. Her mahogany, brown eyes gazed out of a near window and experienced something that her tiny spirit never witnessed before. Payton encountered a new adventure. For the first time, she saw something weightless and clear fall from the heavens and transform everything it touched. She witnessed puddles formulating in the crevices of the Earth and trees swaying to a calmer rhythm.

Watching Payton grow up has been a joy that my heart can't explain. She faithfully finds novelty in so many things that I don't think twice about. Over the course of a few years, I've watched her eyes light up at the sound of shaking keys or the reflection of gold bangles bouncing off a wall. Her world lights up as her exploratory spirit learns, experiences, and appreciates something new.

From the moment she entered the world until now, Payton has taught me something special.

When you've been around something for so long, you get accustomed to its presence. You fail to remember how you felt when you first laid eyes on it and become consumed with it fulfilling its current role in your life. We expect our senses to be there when needed. Yet to someone who is using his or hers for the time, the moment is life changing.

Take time everyday to embrace the ordinary. We live in a society that is constantly moving. Every other day, there is a new product advertising how you can do more in a day than the average human being.

But why would God allow more to transpire in your life when you have failed to value what is currently within your reach?

Dedicate some of your attention to the little things that go unnoticed. Thank God for the blowing of the wind and the drifting of the clouds. Have a date with the sunrise and wink at the moon from time to time. Recognize Him in the green lights as you drive to work or the red ones that kept you from the things that could have happened if you got to where you were going on time. Take a step back and just stand in awe of the little things He's created and permitted to happen in your life. Appreciating the little things will inevitably allow God to grant us with greater things beyond our imagination.

Reflection:

- What are you currently taking for granted?

- If these things were to disappear, how would your life change?

- What changes can you make today to appreciate what God has entrusted you with thus far?

PETAL II
Honesty Hour

My neighbor and I have a very interesting relationship. "John" and I live a hiccup from each other, but our opposing views on life make it seem even further. With the exception of the day of the week the trash goes out, he and I rarely see eye-to-eye on anything. It doesn't matter if it's the weather or the greatest movie of all time, we argue… about everything. However recently, over guacamole and enchiladas, we discussed the controversial topic of dating and relationships. And in the history of our friendship, John found something other than the trash to agree upon.

Somewhere between hopscotch and happy hour, we've lost our urgency to be honest with others and ourselves. As children, our immediate actions stemmed from how we felt at the time. If you liked someone, you told him or her. There was no intimidation or hesitation because the concept was simple: *I like you. You like me. I'm not proposing marriage, but, on the way home, I would like to sit next to you on the bus.* Period.

Today, that very same simplicity is tainted with emotionalism and unnecessary expectations. When we think of someone, we don't call for fear of seeming desperate. When in public, we act as if we don't see that someone to anticipate his or her move first. Instead of vocalizing our anger or expressing how we really feel, we utter those false, fluke, and fickle words to hide the truth: *"I'm okay".*

Last year I embarked upon the epic milestone of turning 30, and in the short amount of time God has given me, I've become more comfortable in my skin than ever before. So when it comes to matters of the heart, here's my theory: *"It's better to express than expect."* The things that were once cute at 15 are no longer adorable at 30. Therefore, speak up on how you feel and go after what you want.

Our expectations sometimes lie in a subconscious idea that someone magically knows how we think and feel and they should act accordingly when in actuality they haven't a clue. Baby steps inevitably lead to walking. How can a toddler cross the finish line hand-in-hand with an infant? The difference between trying and triumph is a little "umph". Make moves towards your desired destination before what you have becomes what you had.

Reflection:

- Why is it difficult disclosing our true feelings to others?

- What façades are you wearing? What are they covering?

- How can you defeat your fears and become more honest with your thoughts, feelings, and actions?

PETAL III
Baggage Claim

Two artists. One message.

In November 2000, the incomparable and iconic Erykah Badu released her most acclaimed and applauded album "Mama's Gun". Badu's intense approach to life, love, and liberty is unmistakably profound through this 14-track compilation. Her classic tune *Bag Lady* illustrates a woman who is in danger of missing her destiny because she refuses to let go of her past. Badu never goes into depth of the things that are weighing this mystery woman down. However, her lyrics create a window of opportunity for her listeners to reevaluate themselves and the luggage they subconsciously carry into the different arenas of their lives.

Fast forward to January 2012: Mr. & Mrs. Shawn Carter give birth to their daughter Blue Ivy.

Jay-Z immediately enters the booth to record one of his most transparent and heartfelt tracks *Glory*. And, of course, the world listens. *Glory* shares very intimate thoughts for Miss Blue from her parents as well as some advice from her dear ole' Dad: *"Make sure the plane you're on is bigger than your carry-on."* Jay-Z uses the illustration of general airport protocol only permitting passengers to have one carry-on bag to accompany them to their destination. The items in this carry-on are important and significant to the flier, ensuring that wherever they are going they will have everything they need, not everything they want or own.

Both artists, though completely different in genre and content, tap into a commonly overlooked theory.

Think of it this way - Imagine you're going on a backpacking trip with your closest friends for a weekend of leisure and an all-around good time. The night before, you realized you haven't packed a thing. You put on some music and get to work packing the things for your anticipated weekend. In theory, you are simply packing necessities. There is no need to bring along every pair of jeans, sneakers, or underwear you own. If you pack in this fashion, there leaves little room for comfort because you have to haul the superfluous weight of your greed along your journey. This is unnecessary packing for two reasons: 1) When you really need something you have packed, you will waste time and energy rummaging through excessive junk you never originally needed, and 2) You won't need everything you own for where you're going.

Badu and Jay-Z make it very plain: Everything isn't meant to accompany you on your journey. Some things are better left behind.

Find some personal time to sift out the things you've been carrying around that bring nothing but dead weight into your space. One of the greatest revelations I've learned is that everything and everyone you encounter should not accompany you for where you're destined to go. It is neither a requirement nor necessity to bring everything and everyone you are connected to along. Badu reminds us that unnecessary baggage will get in your way, while Jay-Z illustrates that your plane won't take off if the plane is too heavy. So as you sort through your luggage, keep in mind that your purpose and destiny aren't a bandwagon or an open invitational for everyone to witness. It's best to leave some things and some people where they belong… behind.

Reflection:

- What baggage are you carrying that is difficult to part from?

- What do you feel you would lose if you left those things or people behind?

- Sift through your life and list three things and/or people you need to separate yourself from and why it is best for you both to part ways.

PETAL IV
Sometimes...

Emotions are as powerful as erupting volcanoes. Whether consciously or not, our emotions dictate many of our behaviors throughout the day. When we don't feel like exercising, we don't. When we feel like eating, we do. But sometimes, our emotions need to give up their shotgun seat in the car of our journey and hop in the trunk until controlled.

While in college, I fell in love with a man who thought no more of me than decorative garnish on a plate of escargot. He meant the world to me. From his suave demeanor to his charismatic laugh, he captivated me. He held my attention in a fashion like no other man I had ever encountered. Yet, his feelings toward me resided on the opposite goalpost on the end zone of love. Our relationship consisted of pleasurable, late night rendezvouses. The magnitude and intensity of this deemed "love" originated behind crème doors, R. Kelly albums, and winter firesides. A drink here and a smoke there, fleeting moments were planned and puffed up to fill a void of loneliness and gloom. This infatuation carried on for years. Why? Because in my twisted reality, I felt like he would (one day) come around. I figured if I remained visible and available, the love I felt for him would be returned. Despite the blatant and evident signs of him not being interested in a relationship and aside from him not pursuing me in the least bit, I had hope.

Hope based on feelings can be dangerous, damaging, and detrimental to any relationship. The inconsistency and instability that feelings create will inevitably flood our minds and cloud our reason. I *hoped* the sky would open, his love for me would transcend through the heavens, and we would embark on a love that would change the hands of time. Needless to say, it didn't happen... and it wasn't his fault. I sold myself dreams based of how I felt when I was with him, not what we were when we were apart. This hope backfired and not only left me lonely, but broken. Instead of discerning the facts surrounding our subconsciously stated agreement, I depended on my feelings to produce a sufficient and substantial relationship, solely because of how I felt.

But, sometimes, we need to forget how we feel and remember what we deserve.

Too often in the lives we're blessed to live, we forget how to live it. We become so consumed with what our present wants rather than what our future needs. We must get ourselves to a place where those temporary moments of satisfaction no longer take the place of our worth. Pat Riley once said, *"Worth is proven by our actions, not our words."* Talk, like a $20 Chanel purse in a New York City alley, is cheap. You can talk yourself until you're blue in the face about the validity of something because it feels right. Yet, the truth lies in the factual accounts of what you see and how you act upon it. In your quest for self-discovery, never neglect the substance of your value. If sand makes you feel grounded, you'll eventually plummet in an abyss of nothingness. Ensure that every deliberate action is orchestrated to shape and mold your most prized, proud, and prominent possession – you.

Reflection:

- Are your actions primarily led by your emotions or your logic?

- How can you ensure the decisions you make are more purposely driven and less emotionally led?

PETAL V
Extreme Makeover

Currently, I work for Maryland's Prince George's County Public School System as a high school English teacher and a Project Coordinator for graduating seniors. A percentage of my seniors must complete and successfully pass an academic project in order to receive their high school diploma. Facilitating these projects goes beyond making sure each project looks presentable, but also certifying whatever is submitted to our county is appropriate and accurate.

My students often go through extensive lengths to make their project look the part. However, sometimes, once reviewed, their submissions are more wrong than leather pants in the summer. They think their scorer will become so captivated by the use of collegiate font and perfect space alignment and completely disregard the impreciseness of their work. A crisp manila folder and fancy typed label means nothing if the content of their project is inaccurate or incomplete. It doesn't matter if the project looks appealing or exquisitely organized. If the quality of what is on the inside of the package isn't acceptable, it is immediately sent back for the student to revise and try again.

Isn't it amazing how much time we spend on how we look than who we are? We will spend countless hours rummaging through closets of clothes, shoes, hats, and bags for an event or typical day to work. From the barbershops and hair salons to department stores and on-line shopping, we don't think twice about the price we'll pay to look amazing. Some will say the more you cater to your outer man, your inner man will have no choice than to comply and follow suit; you'll feel good because you look good.

I disagree.

Now don't get me wrong; a little mascara or shape-up can go a long way. But how you look has absolutely nothing to do with the condition of your heart. As I impress upon my students in reference to their projects, looking the part doesn't compare to the content of the material. It's the content of their work that counts toward their greater good. In the event the inside consists of nonsense, a great deal of effort is made to regroup, revise, and resubmit the original task.

Many of us need a *Core Makeover*, an opportunity to assess what we're facing internally versus the image we are trying to portray externally. Covering up our brokenness, pain, rejection, shame, anxieties, and fears inadvertently turns us into emotional hoarders. Our circumstances knot up in our spirits making it impossible for us to see ourselves for who we really are and the things that boggle us down.

A disguise only lasts but for so long; sooner or later, you'll become exhausted holding it up. Drop the act, start digging, and examine yourself. Rest assure in knowing the gold you will find will be priceless.

Reflection:

- What are some seen or unseen flaws you are hiding?

- How can disregarding these problems affect your life? Spouse? Children? Vision?

- How can you handle these problems before they affect your livelihood?

PETAL VI
Clean It Up

I adore my father. In my eyes, Dr. Tillman R. Sease, Jr. is the most phenomenal, honorable, hard-working, and respectable man in the world. The love he possesses for his family and the compassion he holds for the world is undeniably extraordinary. His wisdom is infinite, and his integrity is immeasurable. But, it took years for me to see him in this light; pride, arrogance, and a lack of humility failed to let me show it.

My father and I held a trying and rather difficult relationship during my high school years. From my life choices to future ambitions, my father and I constantly bumped heads. Between my siblings, I have always been the bull-in-a-china-shop child. I rarely entered a room without the world hearing me first and strived to always have the last word in a heated argument. This, as you would guess, irritated my calm and collected father. I resented him for years for rarely being emotionally sensitive to his rambunctious child. I often felt he favored my younger sister over me and subconsciously wished I possessed more of her reserved and quiet spirit.

I never truly felt accepted by my father growing up. I would sometimes pray and ask God to alter and mutate everything He created me to be in an effort to appease my father's perception of how I *should* be. This umbrella of inadequacy gave birth to endless insecurities, anxieties, and fears throughout my college and adult years. Even while writing this, I'm in tears reminiscing on the moments in my life where I feigned for validation from others, because I felt the one person I reverenced the most despised who I was.

Now, years later, things have dramatically changed for the better with my father and I. As I matured, God opened my eyes to the admirable character of Daddy Dearest. I learned why my father is the way he is. I asked and listened to the stories of his childhood as he shared the hurdles he had no choice but to overcome. I observed how he applied his knowledge of life from one aspect of life to another. I stood in awe of how he lived to uphold his work ethic and how he gave everything he put his mind to his best. The relationship I've gained with my father is one I wouldn't trade for the world. But this change started with an unlikely source…me.

Throughout my life, I've heard various stories concerning parent-child relationships. A large percentage of my friends hold massive amounts of bitterness and anger toward one if not both of their parents for various reasons. Whether for a lack of parental presence or a discovered trail of secrets, they have anchored themselves in their past because of the irreversible decisions and behaviors of their parents. But when does one make a conscious decision toward reconciliation…not for their parents but for themselves?

My beautiful and amazing sister-friend Hana lacks a strong and intimate relationship with her mother. For years, she was kept in the dark from the one person whom she thought would always be a beacon of light. As her life progressed, the absence of her mother grew as well. Yet, instead of remaining in a place of anger and resentment, she consciously chose to not enter another chapter of her life until she found her mother and attempted to heal their relationship. The remarkable effort that Hana has placed into mending their relationship is amazing not only because of the time and energy she has sacrificed, but because, though she didn't cause this rift, she was willing to fix it.

I'm a firm believer that God orchestrates and aligns every intricate detail of our lives for a reason, including the selection of our parents. They play a major role in shaping our identity into the men and women we are destined to become. Regardless of our feelings toward them, we are mandated to honor their position in our lives and not their human nature. I think sometimes we forget the people closest to us are imperfect people, and when those imperfect people hurt us, our wounds outweigh our logic.

My prayer is that you too will make the first step and give life to the skeletons hidden in the closets of your heart for your own healing. When I sought God on how to confront my father on the dying trees that grew from those hurtful roots, God created a window of opportunity for me to address my father in love. To my surprise, God also allowed my father to open up on how I've hurt him as well. Where he hoped I would have listened, observed, and learned lessons from his experiences, he watched me endure great trials and errors simply because I failed to adhere to his wise counsel.

Let this be a season of forward movement for you; a bold and committed stride toward a burden-free future. Fear not those uncomfortable yet courageous conversations or the memories that are bound to surface. Whatever things from your past you've consciously swept under a rug, I implore you to actively take part in some spring-cleaning. The greatest component to healing and restoration is the ability to help someone else who is enduring the same situation. Being healed and being "over it" are two completely different things. Being "over it" simply holds you in captivity of that pain. Healing, on the other hand, is disabling the crutch of pain in order to possess a mindset of peace. This enables us to gain a perspective of wisdom in order to guide someone else in search of his or her own discovery of serenity.

Nana used to say, *"Erin, you can't be a woman in little girl shoes."* I think that message still applies today. Don't allow the circumstances of your past dictate the promise of your future. As rough and soul stirring as that first step towards healing may be, the pay off in the end will be worth it. Be encouraged.

Reflection:

- Describe the relationship you have with your father.

- Describe the relationship you have with your mother.

- How have you contributed to the success or detriment of your relationship with them?

- Where does your relationship with both of your parents need healing?

- What steps can you take to start the reconciliation process?

PETAL VII
Slow & Steady

As I pulled into my driveway from work one afternoon, I saw one of my closest girlfriends waiting for me to get home. Her excitement bolted through my house before I had a chance to put my purse down and turn the alarm off. As I sat on the couch, she paced my living room floor as she told me about "Charles".

Charles, an attorney on Capitol Hill, had approached her a few weeks ago at a popular downtown happy hour. His dashing and debonair charm swept her off her feet...and a few hours later into the sheets of his downtown condo. Days had passed and their quality time consisted of text messages, Chinese take-out, and a daily "roll in the hay". Bubbly and full of hope, she plopped on my couch to hear my thoughts. With love and a large glass of Merlot, I pulled out a verbal AK-47 and demolished whatever majestic dream she was envisioning. Hours later, her dream was deferred and an attitude was born.

There are so many ideas rolling through my mind as I think about the detrimental predicaments my friend constantly and consistently endures. She mentally coordinated her wedding day and chose baby names days after meeting this man, knowing as little as his allergies let alone his middle name. I find it disheartening that so many people, including my dear friend, fall so deeply in lust without encompassing the anticipation of love. It seems as if we want a quick fix to a gradual process.

We live in a day and age where accuracy is contingent upon speed: If it's fast, then it's right. In the past, when you wanted clothes washed, you grabbed soap and a washboard, went to a river, dropped to your knees, and manually washed your garments. When you wanted to express your love and appreciation for someone, you found pen and paper and wrote a letter. When you were hungry, you cooked from one method and from one place: scratch and the heart. Today, these necessities are fulfilled with overpriced appliances, emails, and drive-thru windows. We've lost our sense of patience and replaced it with a desire of urgency. Don't get me wrong: I have embraced the efficiency and effectiveness of technology, but the vast productivity of some things shouldn't replace the skilled and tactful work ethic of others.

One of my closest girlfriends was asked an interesting request of foolery in the early days of 2014. "Samuel" met my friend "Clover" while working on a nearby computer in her cubicle. They sparked a conversation that left Clover rather intrigued. I'm assuming once Samuel felt he had the green light, he pulled out his phone to retrieve Clover's phone number and email address. After a few chit-chats and texts here and there, Samuel created a *Potential Girlfriend Application Form* and eagerly sent it to her in hopes of discovering, based on her answers, if she was worth pursuing. Questions such as *"Have you ever had a sex change"*, *"What's your weight?"*, and *"Do you have a history of mental illness"* are just a few inquisitive components of Samuel's "Need to Know" database. Now here's the thing: I appreciate Samuel wanting to know these and other things. To be honest, he deserved to know all of the answers to the questions he asked of any woman he desires to chase. However, this man has completely misplaced his noodle if he thinks taking the time to get to know her, or any woman for that matter, is replaceable with an unedited Google Doc. When did dating and putting forth effort in building substantial relationships become such a burden? Are you that lazy or is your time that valuable, Sammy Boy, that you can't fathom carving out ample and meaningful time to learn the life of another person?

In the world of relationships, enjoy cultivating the newness. There is something special about getting to know someone different for the first time. From their hobbies and food interests to family dynamics and personal goals, the status of the future rests on the stability of the present. Strive to develop meaningful relationships with people by creating ample time to learn who they are. Unlike Rosetta Stone, there is no fast way to learn someone's character. Slow down, take your time, and enjoy valuing the movement before it passes you by.

Reflection:

- Is it difficult getting to know someone new? Why or why not?

- How can patience build the validity of relationships?

- **Answer whichever applies:**
    a) If you're single, how can you be patient and content while you're waiting on your mate?

    b) If you're dating or married, how can you spend more time getting to know your significant other?

PETAL VIII
Time-Out Corners

In March of 2012, I celebrated my 29th birthday. To my students' surprise, their beloved English teacher was not turning the 23 or 25 they hoped, but walking into her last "20 something".

Through the course of my life, I have always looked forward to my birthday. From the unique theme to the exquisite pre-ordered cake, I had always taken pleasure in the concept of planning my special day from start to finish. Whether a getaway with the girls or a simple dinner with close family and friends, my birthday celebration was a never-ending, anticipated event…but not this year.

On a Saturday afternoon in mid-January, I sat around my mother's kitchen table for our weekly chat over tea and treats when she said something that sent chills down my spine. *"Girl, you've run out of twenties. Thirty will be here before you know it."* I cringed as my heart sunk to the bottom of my stomach. Filled with sadness and disbelief, reality kicked in as I realized that in a year I would be entering another decade. My 20s were officially over and this new age would illustrate what I had done with my life thus far. Needless to say, I wasn't pleased.

As most young girls, we plan our lives from beginning to end. We strategically jot down the details of our careers, finances, relationships, and social lives. I know I'm not the only one who has mentally designed their dream house, planned their dream wedding, and had their desired amount of kids all while living in their dream city. The problem here lies within: our fascination was solely based on a fantasy while neglecting our present reality.

As I embarked on this new age, I realized I wasn't where I thought I would be. I never studied abroad. I didn't have a fulfilling career. I wasn't married let alone in a committed relationship. I hadn't birthed any children or was pursued by a man to plan any with. I hadn't moved out of Maryland and I wasn't as financially comfortable as I had hoped. For weeks, I had played a sad tune on my own philharmonic violin as I reminisced about how I spent my 20s. Ten years seemed to have flown by faster than a G5, and I subconsciously felt I wasted them all. The list of shoulda, coulda, woulda's consumed my mind and weighed upon my heart making this year's birthday every bit of unbearable.

And then, God put me in timeout.

I'm a fervent believer that when God speaks to us individually, it's done in a way that is specifically geared towards you; meaning there is no confusion of who's talking when He speaks. For some it's soft whispers. For others, it's through various signs. However, when God speaks to me, He uses time-out corners. It's as if He's pointing His finger to a corner of conviction, sits me in a chair, instructs me to face the wall, and do nothing but listen. So I walked, I sat, I stared, and I listened. And this is what He said:

So let Me get this straight: You're unhappy because you're not where you thought you would be, because where I have you isn't good enough? I've basically made a mistake in bringing you this far and you're still not happy because of things you don't have or places you haven't been...yet? You're pissed because of what you're lacking despite the reasons I've kept you from it.
That's dumb.

God sure does know how to humble the prideful. The Academy Award winning performance I was giving was unmerited and unwanted. I was stuck in a posture of pity rather than perspective of praise and, needless to say, God wasn't impressed. In that much needed pow-wow with the Man upstairs, I grew a little wiser and learned two amazing things:

1. Sometimes, you have to rejoice in the things God didn't bring to pass.
Truth be told, as much as I desired (and still do) a relationship, marriage, and children, at no point in my 20s was I ready for all the things that came with. I was mesmerized with this image of perfection in my head yet fearful of never growing old with someone to experience it with. My friends were falling in love, getting married, having children, and moving forward with their lives and I felt like I was running through quicksand trying to keep up. But none of the men I dated in my 20s were worth an "I do," and at no point in time could I handle or support a child coming into the world.

2. Many of the things we desire never occur because of a lack of effort on our part.
I truly believe that we play a role in the things we aspire to become and hope to obtain. However, we can't sit and wait for things to fall from the sky, land in our lap, and leave the work to the universe. If it's a career, an opportunity to travel, a dream, or a vision, make moves to get the ball rolling; it won't roll itself. When God made you, He was fully aware of *how* He made you. You embody the strength and ambition to succeed at whatever you set your mind to. However, your mind shouldn't be the only thing moving. Empower yourself to disregard fear, step out on faith, and make confident strides toward your goals.

I was reminded that where I was may not have been the way I planned it, but I was precisely where God wanted me to be. His placement was, is, and will always be perfect. Be grateful for His positioning and the things that God allows in your life, but also delight yourself in the things you're not facing and the things He didn't allow to occur. He knows best, so trust Him. He really knows what He's doing, and at no point in time will He ever need your personal consultations.

Wherever you are and whatever season you're in, make it a point to appreciate the moment before criticizing how it contradicts your vision. There is a lesson in everything, and in anything worth having, a test is soon to follow. Yet, if you're not paying attention in your class of life and disregarding the warnings of the Teacher, don't expect greatness, for your grade is contingent upon your effort.

Reflection:

- Are you content with where you are or trying to catch up to where you thought you would be?

- What are the innermost desires of your heart?

- What are your short/long-term goals? If faith without works and effort is dead, what are you doing to bring your vision to life?

PETAL IX
Lingering Lattes

On an impromptu visit to Starbucks, I came across two "girls" engaged in a heated discussion. In a duel between their tone and the espresso machine, loyal patrons of this beloved haven couldn't help but take notice as well. As I waited in the molasses-moving line, I couldn't help but overhear the gist of their intense and inappropriate conversation.

Girl #1 complained about her good-for-nothing boyfriend who apparently was as dumb as a doorknob. As steamed flowed from her nostrils, Girl #2 chimed in about her fiancé's impotence and insensitive ways. Whether these fellas weren't idolizing them for the queens of the Earth they considered themselves to be or weren't responding fast enough to their beckoned calls, needless to say, these "girls" detested their men.

Let me paint this picture for you as lucidly as I can: Two "girls" in their mid-30s, who apparently failed the *Indoor vs. Outdoor Voice* quiz in kindergarten, blatantly and disrespectfully transformed Starbucks from a mecca of tranquility into a catty carry-out in order to grumble and gripe about their love lives. *[NOTE: I continue to refer to these females as "girls" because women don't do this. There is an art to class that only real women understand].* Here's a sample of the injustice my ears and latte witnessed:

> *"Why hasn't he proposed yet?"*
> *"My ex was smarter than him."*
> *"Girl you know he can't hit it right, either."*
> *"If I aint feel sorry for him, I woulda been dump him by now."*
> *"He is such a little boy."*

How can you supersede the noise of a coffee machine by degrading the man in your life in hopes of him putting a ring on your finger? Are you really discussing the ins and outs of your sex life for the caffeine citizens of America to hear? Was this an untelevised episode of Punk'd?

It's one thing to vent about a bad day, monthly menstrual cramps, and even the latest social media trend to your girlfriends in hopes of seeking a slither of clarity. However, it is a completely different scenario to have a public, Ping-Pong, male-bashing session, humiliating the character and integrity of YOUR man in front of someone who has no more common sense than an abandoned shoelace.

As a single woman, I have grown to treasure my opposite gender. There is something undeniably remarkable about a man. To be entrusted by God to have the title of "man" is worth reverencing. The responsibility that comes within this territory extends further than feminine logic. Before any of us were born, our gender was already preselected. Your opinion, perspective, or belief as of what you should be was never taken into consideration. I truly believe that one of the factors taken into account of the gender you would fulfill was based on what your life could handle. Therefore, you are what you are because you couldn't handle being the other. So it amazes me to hear women blatantly cast down a figure they don't understand.

Here are two thoughts that made their way into my mind as "Frick & Frack" continued their immature banter:

1. Night & Day:
Men and women are as different as the French and Chinese languages. We spend endless time and energy trying to communicate to each other in our own language while the other has no idea what we're talking about. We grow flustered and frustrated because neither can see the things that logically makes sense to the other.

The interesting thing here is that French will never be Chinese and vice versa. However, through time and patience, one can learn the basics of their counterpart's language. In other words, women will never fully understand men, nor will men ever fully comprehend the essence of women. Yet, through cultivated time and heartfelt patience, the two can learn to coexist. The problem lies when we exhaust ourselves with trying to turn the other into what we think they should become. Sometimes women will make it nearly impossible for their man to "pick their battles" because a woman's emotionalism can turn everything into a Trojan war. Meanwhile, men will at times shut down and seek places of solitude to further confine their thoughts instead of being a wellspring of verbal communication for their lady.

We need to accept the inevitable fact that our genders will forever be different, but when it comes to relationships, groom who you are individually so that you both can grow collectively.

2. Silence is Golden:

Denzel Washington plays Frank Lucas in the 2007 critically acclaimed film *American Gangster*. My favorite line in this movie is *"The loudest one in the room is the weakest one in the room."* A loud woman who complains and slanders her man in public is like UGG boots in the summer – foul. I've been that woman who dishes out all of her dirty laundry about her man to her girlfriends and it eventually left me speechless, shameful, and single. Instead of voicing your opinion to anyone who would listen, discern effective council.

Whatever issues are bothering you in your relationship, handle it in your relationship. Its substance and stability should not be publicized front-page news. Nana used to say, *"Clean your laundry in your house, not the driveway."* Deck out whatever problems you have with your mate within your relationship and if you can't reach a common understanding, seek mediation from a wiser and seasoned couple.

Though my latte experience was ruined, I learned so many things. Prayerfully, Girl #1 and Girl #2 come across this reflection and make an effort to get their men back. If not, I'm more than certain those men left with no intentions of ever returning home.

Reflection:

- In your relationships with others, do you find yourself addressing your problems head-on or venting to anyone who will listen?

- What changes can you make to strengthen the maturity of your relationships?

PETAL X
Rerouting

On a random weekend in April, my homegirl "Josie" and I went on an early hunt for Mothers' Day gifts. While in route to Mazza Gallerie, she began to share her latest irritation with her supervisor. Now if you knew this particular friend of mine, you would know that she loves everything and everyone. Though very few people reside on her "hit-list", the number one victim on this petite roster was her "She-Devil" of an employer.

Josie began to vent how the condescending nature and awful ladylike behavior of her employer was beginning to irritate her more than seasonal cicadas. From her unsuitable attitude to obvious lack of appreciation for her staff, her boss was reverenced more when she was on travel than in her own office. Josie had reached her "hold my tongue" limit and released her frustration like bazooka ammunition.

I empathized with her situation because I've been there. I think we all have had that one boss *(maybe more)* that you secretly hope trips up a flight of stairs or gets a paper-cut in the middle of their back that stings the hell out of them when they hop in the shower. Some employers micromanage their team; refusing to stay in their lane, they hopscotch their way into yours, overshadowing the assignment they've entrusted into your care. Some employers are *Busy-Bees* with their wings in everyone else's pot, while neglecting the honey in their own. Others are so consumed with basking in the light of leadership, they forget to actually lead. In the middle of her rant, I was reminded of something my beloved Pastor mentioned that never left the haven of my mind.

You will never fully like or love everything about someone, especially your employer. They will say and/or do things that will make you want to spit fire of every expletive word in your memory bank. However, if you are doing your job unto your boss, you will never find peace where you earn a living. When we work for someone and place our hope in his or her approval, we will forever be disappointed because humans are fickle. Our emotions ride Six Flags rollercoasters every day, leaving us to never know what highs or lows they're on from one minute to the next. When we lose sight of the evident fact that people are human, we become quickly moved by their imperfections.

Instead of diligently and faithfully working for an erratic human, work unto and toward a faultless and perfect God. Get to work on time… for God. Nail every task that comes across your desk…for God. Genuinely speak and show love to the people rooting against you…for God. If He blessed you with the job, regardless of the sifting seasons it puts you through, honor Him by giving your best every time you set foot there.

Pray for your boss with a heart that desires God to meet them where they are, not to appease how you feel. When we redirect our energy toward the only One who can cause a shift in our working atmosphere, our very own maturity begins to grow. When you're faithful to God, He'll be faithful to you. If your desire is to work somewhere else for someone else, keep this in mind: God won't give you more if you're not faithful in working thoroughly, attentively, and meticulously with what you already have where you already are.

Reflection:

- What are some things that irritate you about your employer/ authority?

- What are some ways to redirect the hostility or irritation you have toward your employer/authority?

PETAL XI
That Ugly Part of Me

For Aaron, Danielle, Crystal, and Trish…thank you.

Imagine you have an appetite for your favorite dessert. Whether German chocolate cake, tiramisu, or a Frosty from Wendy's, at the present time you are craving the delectable taste of your sweet tooth's fantasy. You envision your pursuit of it. The hunt. The chase. You fascinate over its smell, its flavor, even its digestion into your system. The effort placed into the creation of this treat overpowers you. Nevermind its calories or negation of the extensive workout you had at the gym earlier. Nothing, and I mean *nothing* will stand in the way of you and capturing what you yearn for.

That's how I feel about sweets…and lust.

There are some problems and ironies that play a part in both of these struggles. The first is a medical problem. In August of 2011, I was diagnosed with polycystic ovarian syndrome (PCOS), an unfortunate branch of Type 2 Diabetes. PCOS is a hormonal disorder among women of reproductive age where numerous cysts, similar to the shape of a pearl, appear along the outer edge of each ovary. Causes of PCOS range from irregular or prolonged menstrual cycles, insulin resistance, obesity and/or irregular weight gain, acne, and infertility. The blessing in PCOS is that, through diet adjustments and daily exercise, this condition can be reversed. As great as that it is, I still love my sweets. Some people struggle with sweets because they're emotional eaters; they need desserts to have a level of fulfillment or reach a place of happiness. Not me; I just crave the savoring experience.

The second is a spiritual problem. After some extensive research, late night tears, and difficult self-examination, I've reached the conclusion that I'm not a sex addict. I'm not, nor have ever been the kind of person to be intimate with anything that has a pulse. I'm not a subscriber of pornography or patron of prostitution. My list of partners isn't long or embarrassing. I am fully capable of living my life for extended periods of time without engaging in the act of sexual activity and can consume my thoughts throughout the day with things other than this struggle. But, my sexual appetite and its fulfillment are undeniably irregular and indisputably abnormal.

Ironically, though they have no connection to each other, both, I'm certain, play a major part in my destiny. I can honestly say that these struggles have held me bound for quite some time. While one deteriorates my health, the other depreciates my soul. Yet, in the grander scheme of things, they both, if not controlled, will inevitably ruin my purpose. If I continue to live my life fulfilling the desires of a weakening moment, my life will fatally suffer.

Though residing in separate abodes, both struggles have provided great insight on how to care for your outer and inner man simultaneously, but more importantly, effectively:

1. Hey You – Seeing yourself for the real you, are both liberating and frightening encounters. It's easy depicting the life you want others to see. It's simple to render a façade or live out a fantasy because you are able to anticipate its response. Unfortunately, this behavior transforms us into picturesque liars, tiresomely captivating people with false pretenses of who we are. But, at the end of the day, when the mask has no choice but to come down, you can't hide from the *real* you. Though these ugly and shameful things may not have come to light, as of yet, they're nevertheless evermore present. The question is when will you grow tired of camouflaging them. Peel back those layers and shine light on those dark places. Just like a newborn seeing light for the first time, it will hurt and be highly uncomfortable. It will sting, and you will want to retreat back to the way it used to be. Face it head on and reintroduce yourself to yourself.

2. Sister's Keeper – In an effort to stay focused on this new path of self-discovery, it's vital to have at least one person designated to hold you accountable. Once I had completed my "peeling process", I charged two emphatic and assertive ladies in place to hold me accountable in both arenas of my life. What made them so significant and perfect for this assignment was their faithfulness in being there whenever I needed. If I found myself wanting to slip up and give into my flesh, they would literally drop whatever they were doing to save me from myself. Accountability isn't intended to be a leisurely experience. It is an ongoing test of trial and error. Yet, it is made easier to endure when you are willing to have someone keep you on track if and when you grow weary.

3. Gold Stars – My dear friend LaTrisha is one of the greatest advocates and supporters on this side of the Mississippi. From an Olympic race to a bird hatching from an egg, Trish will cheer for almost anything if it is monumental to her friends. Knowing my struggle, where I was, and the destination I had ahead, Trish rooted for me at the end of every week when I successfully made it through seven days of fighting my demons. Even throughout the week, she would recognize my determination and offer endless motivation to make it through the week ahead. Her reassurance helped me find ways to encourage myself. After each week, as a way of patting myself on the back, I would treat myself to a little something for making it through. My first week of consistent exercise and abstinence was rewarded in a matinee movie. Week two was a pair of shoes, and week three was an outdoor jazz concert. As the weeks and now months have progressed, these well-earned gold stars serve as reminders that self-control is doable and manageable. Being able to uplift yourself makes the rewarding all the more worthwhile because no one understands the depth of your struggle and the extent of your fight like you. Therefore, celebrate and delight yourself in your small victories; you deserve it!

In the military, after a smoke grenade is released, a smokescreen appears. Infantries use smokescreens in order to conceal movement and tactics from their enemies. But once the smoke clears, the infantry becomes visible and loses their defense mechanism. The exposure of their infantry comprises the unit, leaving the members of the unit vulnerable to their enemy. Your smokescreens may confine your struggle, but the smoke will eventually clear, leaving you face to face with the very thing you were trying to hide. Avoid becoming your own enemy and purposefully fight to overcome the inner war within yourself.

Reflection:

- What is something you are presently internally battling?

- How does it affect your livelihood?

- If you don't pull your struggle under control, how do you think your purpose and destiny may be affected?

- Start your "peeling process", locate a set of accountability partners, and start tracking your progress. Remember: Take it one day at a time. If at first you don't succeed, dust yourself off and try again. You can do this!

PETAL XII
Streams in Unknown Deserts

As stated in previous entries, my current occupation is a high school educator for Prince George's County, Maryland. Teaching high school students is definitely a bittersweet profession. Between the *I'm grown* attitudes, constant opposition of authority battles, and occasional inactive parents, the bitter moments often make teachers dread that inevitable drive to work day after day. These moments often blur our "this is why I teach" perspective and resentment begins to rear its ugly head through the halls of our classrooms. Yet once the storm has passed and the sun peeks through the clouds, every teacher has that "sweet" moment when they're reminded *why* they do *what* they do. So, after six years of teaching an interesting generation, I was rather surprised and relieved when my personal "ah-ha" moment had finally arrived.

Bladensburg High School conducted its 2012 commencement ceremony on a beautiful Wednesday morning in June. As my babies crossed the burning sands into adulthood, I began to reminisce on the joy and pain I endured to help get them to this point. I remember praying as they began this next chapter of their lives, hoping they would walk in their greatness and pursue excellence regardless of the inevitable circumstances life would lay before their feet. Once the ceremony was over, they tossed their caps effortlessly in the air and left the arena knowing whatever they set their mind to do was possible.

And then it happened.

As I helped my colleague pack up last minute signs, folders, and diplomas, a few students surrounded me in the parking lot claiming that a parent was looking for me. Moments later, a frantically crying mother appeared in my eyesight, threw her arms around me, and said the words I will never forget: *"Ms. Sease you don't know me, but I just wanted to say 'Thank You' for keeping my son out of jail or a coffin."* Needless to say, I lost it. And in that parking lot on that Wednesday morning, I held that mother close and cried right along with her.

She was right…I had no idea who she was. I didn't know her face or her story. Yet a series of events have had to occur within her household that made it impossible to foresee her child graduating from high school this day. Her story must have been filled with heartache and frustration as, through her tears, she poured out her heart of gratitude in my arms. I imagined flashes of the sacrifices she had to make and the mountains she had to climb crossed her mind as she watched her son become a man that morning. She could have embraced any other staff member, counselor, administrator or friend of her son's school, but she searched through hundreds of people to find Ms. Sease.

After we dried our eyes and went our separate ways it dawned on me that I never discovered her name or that of her son. I was totally distraught because I had no idea who this woman or her child was that I affected, but then God showed up and shared something powerful with me.

This woman lived in fear that her son would lose his life to the foolishness of his generation. Evidently, she was tired and worn out. Yet, something I did or said motivated her son to push himself towards his potential. I had no idea that I held the assignment of helping her son through a period in his life that kept him not only ambitious and driven, but also free from imprisonment or a funeral home. In the midst of those bitter moments where I wanted to choose another career path, God reminded me that where I am is not about me…it never was. From the day I was born, God strategically aligned every move I made to not only become an educator, but to cross paths with this young man. This unknown kid needed me to survive and I needed him to remain in God's will.

We will never know the extent of the ripples we have on the lives of those we meet. And sometimes, in an effort to keep us humble and consistent in molding our individual craft, we're not supposed to know. Therefore, it makes it imperative for us to become deliberately conscious of our interaction with everyone we come in contact with. Whether bitter or sweet, there, in the reaction to our actions, lies a purpose. Trust and believe, the aggravating and arduous moments will inevitably occur. Yet, whether in our career, ministry, or even relationships, we must develop a mentality to plant our feet and refuse to retreat when those bitter moments kick in. Our valley moments, though deep and trying, become a designated conduit for others to achieve a level of greatness in their lives. Sometimes the success of others is contingent upon our sorrows. Likewise, our victory is intended for another to become victorious.

Push through those times of adversity, for you don't know who's thriving from your strength.

Reflection:

- Are you conscious of the ripple effects you have on the people you come in contact with?

- If yes, who are the people affected by the life you live?

- If no, how can you become more conscientious of the people, known and unknown, who cross your path?

PETAL XIII
An Ode to Coverings

Recently, I ended an emotional and sensitive slump of the blues. For weeks, I had been feeling lonely, unfulfilled, and inadequate. My days seemed to be passing by and yet running together all at once. I lacked the desire to write or spend time with anyone. My ambition and work ethic began to decline and I started to resent everything and everyone around me. My "funk" was even more noticeable as I began to unconsciously take my anger and frustration out on my family and friends. I could literally go from zero to ten and back to zero in an instant as my mind began to flood with the emptiness I felt inside.

On a random Saturday evening, my best friend Crystal invited me over for an impromptu *Family Night*. Family Night typically consists of our closest friends getting together to talk, laugh, and most importantly, empower one another as we walk hand-in-hand throughout our own personal journeys. To be completely honest, due to this season of gloom, I wasn't feeling it. Although I love my friends and Family Night more than anything on the planet, I wasn't in the mood to bond or socialize with anyone. To remove myself from the comforts of my boyfriend (my couch) and drive 30 minutes away wasn't on my "To Do" list that Saturday evening. My plan was to sit in the house, eat honey wheat pretzels, and watch the Indiana Jones Marathon on TBS. Nevertheless, I peeled myself from my boo, threw on anything (literally), and headed up the road for what turned out to be just what I needed…a refill.

The night kicked off when my girlfriend LaTrece pulled me aside in search of what was happening in the world drifting around in my head. After prolonging her with the *"Girl, I'm fine"* statements and the tug of war between myself and my tears, I finally chose to let loose and pour my heart out to her.

Through the tears and fumbling over my moon-bounced thoughts, I began to notice that over the years, I poured out my heart for everyone and anyone, anytime and anywhere. I had stood in the gap for everyone and interceded on their behalf as often as possible. Due to love, compassion, mercy, and authentic concern, I had given my entire being to people and their needs. I'd lost sleep, peace, and sanity. My world had become this constant waterfall; pouring into people and being a consistent "yes" woman. But now, I was empty. I gave incessantly and now had nothing to show for it but exhaustion and resentfulness. I had nothing to give to myself. All of my energy and desire was scattered into the universe to the point where I couldn't even pray, encourage, or love on myself. Needless to say, I was tired.

Seconds later, Josh, another best friend of mine, not knowing what LaTrece and I just discussed, noticed these hues of blues I was drowning in and offered much needed support and compassion. He could see the effects of this heavy-burdened season and planned that night to confront me on it. Ironically, he stated word for word what I was going through and shared what a poor job I was doing in trying to keep it together. He knew that I spent the majority of my life being the ever-present helping hand to the world while not taking care of myself and now my serenity was paying for it.

I was speechless as I shed uncontrollable tears in Crystal's kitchen surrounded by the people who loved me the most. I couldn't believe the evident confirmation God created that night. I had been trying to keep it together for so long, but my family saw right through my mask. Each individual in that kitchen knew how much of myself I had given to insignificant people and pointless things but failed to take into vast consideration my heart, soul, and mind. For fear of being deemed selfish, I put myself on the backburner and forgot I was there.

Sometimes, God creates blankets of people to cover us in our seasons of despair. Their purpose is to show you the side of yourself you neglect to see. They serve as tour guides of how to maneuver around stumbling blocks instead of bumping into them. Their love is tough and meant to sting you back into reality. The special gift in a covering is knowing there is always someone willing to fight for you when your strength gives out. They understand you are not an infinite-operating machine; that, every now and then, you will need to be replenished and refueled for your own sanity. What I love about these coverings is that not just anybody can occupy this position. They are fashioned by God to play vital roles on the stage of your life. Without them, your story lacks plot and substance.

Take time to recognize and honor the coverings in your life. Thank them for wrapping significant time in their lives around yours and knowing what's best for you when your world seems hectic and unclear. You need them to survive, so thank them for reminding you how to live.

Reflection:

- Where in your life are you over-extending yourself?

- Of your friends and family, who pours into you when you're running on fumes?

- How can you make more time to get refilled with what you need after you fulfill the needs of others?

PETAL XIV
The Makings of You

Earlier this year, an old high school friend invited me to tag along to a jewelry store in hopes of helping him shop for an engagement ring. I eagerly agreed as he brought me along to witness the extraordinary piece he picked out for his future bride. While my friend finalized details with his jeweler, my lack of an attention span kicked in and I began to explore the breathtaking rings on display. Those who are well acquainted with my social life are fully aware that I can make friends with a rock if the conversation is decent. However, instead of Earth's accessory, I made a friend in the extraordinary jewelry appraiser "Mark".

My newly found best friend Mark told me that a woman's engagement ring should fit not just her personality but also her experience. Captivated by this new outlook on ring shopping, I let Mark explain the essence in the connection between a diamond and a woman:

"The flawlessness of a diamond is cultivated on two things: heat and pressure. The size of a diamond is contingent upon the intensity of heat and pressure. Therefore, the creation of a small carat diamond is different from that of a larger carat diamond because it cannot handle the process. So, if you ever come across a massive diamond that makes your heart skip a beat and halt the motion of time, honor it for a moment not simply for its beauty, but for everything it went through to get there."

Ladies and Gentlemen, for the first time, I introduce to some and present to others the diamond in my life, Madeline Mobley Sease… my mother.

I'm not certain of a lot of things. I don't know the distance between the Earth and the sun. Besides the recorder in the fifth grade and "Hot Crossed Buns", I can't play an instrument or read sheet music. I've never got anything higher than a C- in chemistry, and I can't speak another language. However, if I am certain and confident of one thing it is this: there is no greater or stronger woman on the Earth than my mother. I could spend eternity listing the various qualities that intrigue me about my mother, but there will never be a space large enough to contain my fascination. She is a woman of infinite compassion, mercy, and grace. However, the ultimate attribute of my mother that inspires me each and everyday are her constant efforts to maintain her optimism despite her obstacles.

"Ma Sease" practically raised herself. From watching her mother scrub floors and clean homes for families, caring for a drug addicted brother, fighting through life-threatening situations, enduring deception from those closest to her, my mother proved there is life beyond the valley. Her drive and work ethic put her through school. Her humble and kind spirit postured her to be pursued by the love of her life. Her patience produced three beautiful children and established a rewarding and fulfilling career within the DC and Maryland Educational System. The mountain she stands on now is a testament that her view is tangible, but it will cost a heap of heat and painful pressure.

My mother's life epitomizes a monumental belief. The journey she had to travel to arrive at this juncture is incredible. She has been betrayed, double-crossed, and misled. She had to learn how to nurture and comfort herself the majority of her life and learn lessons solely from falling flat on her face first. Her life illustrates the infamous mantra that God will never give us more than we can bear. Therefore, whatever is presented to you, you have the strength to withstand anything.

Often times when faced with adversity, we are keen to surrender to the tension of our situation than sustain the trial. There were hundred of moments in my mother's life when she could have thrown in the towel and given up the fight. Yet, I'm convinced when her back was against the wall and she felt there was no one in her corner, she endured her assigned heat and pressure, convinced that her discomfort would eventually lead to a purpose-driven victory.

My dear friend Melanie Belton always says, *"Anything worth having must be tested by fire."* If our tests require flames, we mustn't run at the sight of smoke. The foremost ingredients of heat and pressure formulate the refinement of one's character. My mother has proven the heat and pressure process is worth it, for though it wasn't the path she chose, she honors it as being the will of God. It is only through the courage and tenacity to stare fear in the face that not only creates elite integrity but also enables one to endure the inescapable sifting seasons.

In baseball, pitchers throw batters curveballs in an effort of distraction from hitting the ball. Successful pitching maneuvers not only make the pitcher an asset to their team, but a challenge to the opposing one. Therefore, the batter must strategize tactics to manipulate the curveballs in order to earn a victory for their team.
The world has a way of reeling curveballs at our plate of life. It seems as if just when our stance is stable, something trips us back into the dugout. However, life will also equip us with tools to dust ourselves off and try again. Strengthen yourself to do so.

Reflection:

- What is your current test?

- Who in your life has endured an intensive test? What lesson(s) did they learn from that experience?

- How can you live more optimistically through your current test?

PETAL XV
Mic Check 1,2…1,2

I'm not a chick-flick kind of girl. From the endless overflow of tears to "getting in touch with one's feelings", I've always despised the use of excessive Kleenex while watching a movie. Give me an Italian mob family, a mythological epic, or a plot with an unseen twist and I'm in cinema heaven. However, every woman has that one movie you pray is televised on *Lifetime* on a rainy afternoon. As you switch from channel to channel, you subconsciously hope that one film is scheduled on someone's network so you can mentally retreat to a place where communicating with the outside world becomes nonexistent and undesirable. And within that all-time favorite film, as we recite those priceless one-liners and anticipate the "I've seen this part over 100 times" scenes, we tend to gravitate towards that one character our hearts simply adore and fascinate over.

For me, this film is *Steel Magnolias* and that character is played by the incomparable Shirley MacLaine as "Louisa Ouiser *(pronounced Weeza)* Boudreaux". In 1989, director Herbert Ross directed one of the most groundbreaking films of all time in hopes of illustrating that while women may be delicate as a flower, the trials and life-altering circumstances they inevitably face make them strong as steel. All of the women in this film were just that: sensitive on the outside and bulletproof strong on the inside…except for Ouiser. Ouiser was blunt, straightforward, and to the point. Very rarely did she speak to appease anyone. She didn't care how much money you had or the prominence of your position in your career. Words were the ammunition to her ruthless-toned bazooka. She spoke her mind at all costs in a way that made others uneasy and highly uncomfortable.

Ouiser and I are long lost sisters.

Over the past year, I have been confronted by four of my closest friends in reference to the things I say and how I say them. I have what's called a 99-P (99.9% Problem). Ninety-nine percent of the time, I'm adamant about how I feel and stand strongly to what I have to say. If asked or prompted, if you're wrong, foul, or out of line, I will tell you. In a heated discussion, it goes without saying that I will always stand by my opinion. Never will I feel an urge to yell or step out of character in any given situation, but the darts of words that spring from my heart cause fatal blows. Yet the remaining 1% holds the best, yet unseen, intentions. Like Ouiser, the goal is not to hurt someone or destroy their pride but to get my point across so all parties involved are on the same page. However, when my tone kicks in, that honest objective is overshadowed by my lack of compassion and understanding.

In kindergarten, I learned a simple mantra: *"Honesty is the best policy"*. I assumed my teacher desired to lay the first brick in building stable and solid integrity in her students. For the man or woman who desires to use this policy in their adulthood, that same belief lies at the forefront of our minds when confronted with various people and situations; that there can be no harm in being honest with yourself and others. Yet, even though honesty and nobility are character traits we all desire, when expressing our views and opinions, two things come to mind:

1. The Off Switch: Everyone doesn't need to know how you think and feel **all** the time. Just because you're cognizant of your thoughts and feelings does not require the world to have that same awareness. A mature adult is able to discern when their voice is required and when their silence is desired. Sometimes, silence is the best shift maker a situation needs. Ask God to create opportunities and platforms for you to speak and share your voice with others, as well as learning when to give your vocal cords a rest.

2. The Tower of Power: Imagine you've just arrived to work. You sit at your desk, sip your coffee, and begin the duties of the day. Suddenly, your boss enters your space and says something to you that makes your blood boil. It's as if fire spewed from their pores and singed everything in sight. You then realize it's not what your boss said but how he/she said it. Often times we may express ourselves in a way that aligns itself with that previously stated honesty policy. However, the receiver of your delivery may grow offended by your use of tone. The tongue is the driving force behind the words we speak. If there is power in our words, we must be conscious enough to choose to speak life to everyone in our midst. It takes seconds to tear someone down, but it will take a lifetime for that person to emotionally trust you again. Gain a filter before it costs you the vulnerability of your family and friends.

I love Ouiser, for the fictitiousness of her character is a vast comedic relief from the everyday world. However, I don't live in a fantasy or a dramatic comedy. As life carries on, there are no cuts, replays, stand-ins or stunt doubles to take my place. Making everyday count goes beyond fulfilling your needs, but that of others as well. Be the sound you want to hear before more is muted than your voice.

Reflection:

- Is the delivery of your honesty always the best policy? Why or why not?

- Who have you offended, hurt, or scarred because of your tone/words?

- How can you start today to mend what's been broken in an attempt to fix that relationship?

PETAL XVI
Preoccupied Porcupines

In December 2012, I had the opportunity to portray a Biblical figure in my church's annual Christmas production. I was given three
weeks to research, study, and ultimately become the *Woman with the
Issue of Blood*. For years, I learned about this woman and her condition. Biblically, she was a young adult woman who suffered a form
of vaginal hemorrhaging. For twelve years, she was held in exile from
her community. During this time in history, when a woman experienced her monthly menstrual cycle, she also endured the physical
and emotional separation from her family and friends. Women during their "time of the month" were considered to be unclean and
therefore shunned from their society. Day after day, she sought healing for her condition and, without fail, was faithfully turned away.
Yet, with every new morning, she embarked each day with a greater
and more empowered sense of hope to be healed from her impurity.
It was only through a leap of faith, when she heard Jesus would be
in town, that she pressed her way through a forceful crowd, reached
to touch the hem of His garment, and was instantly healed from her
infirmity.

I was honored and privileged to represent this woman. I wanted
my depiction of her to be perfect, sound, and believable. However,
through a week of intense rehearsal with my acting mentor, the un-
believable happened: I lost my voice. Whatever voice I had one moment was now replaced by a husky lumberjack the next.

Production time is always an intense time; there is literally never a
stress-free moment. Between my director managing an entire cast,
overseeing staging, cueing lights and music, directing lead roles,

assisting lines, and gelling every seen and unforeseen component into a memorable and phenomenal show, the last thing he needed was his stage manager and co-finale closer to lose her voice. I instantly diagnosed myself with laryngitis, stalked every medical website online, and became obsessed with getting my voice back in time for opening night. The local CVS pharmacist knew me by face and name as I wiped out his Cold & Flu section. But with all of my efforts, bottomless green teas, Chloraseptic sprays, throat coats, and Hot Toddy's, my voice never returned by show time.

And then it happened. God, as He so unashamedly does, put me in time out... yet again.

On the morning of our first show, I was preparing my DIY concoctions when God showed up in my kitchen. I was asked a simple question that brought uncontrollable tears to my eyes and forced me to my knees. With a convicted heart, I heard God ask, *"Why are you obsessed with perfection and not prepared for ministry?"* Talk about a rude awakening. Ironically, though I had no voice during all three shows, as soon as I set foot on that stage, God invoked *something* to come from my mouth. Though I had no voice, He showed up to give me what I needed: a voice that was effective and purposeful for the moment He designed.

Sometimes, what vexes us in life is the image in our head of how we think things are supposed to be. We think we should live *this* way, dress *this* way, drive *this* car, make *this* amount of money, work in *this* career, marry *this* spouse, and have *this* type of life. But I'm thoroughly convinced that when our thoughts encircle themselves in what we think, God hysterically laughs at our plans.

Flawlessness is unattainable by anyone. It doesn't matter how much blood, sweat, and tears we put into something, there will always be a pinnacle of perfection we will never reach. Yet in the solidified purpose in our innate beings, God steps in and allows our imperfections to be a blessing to someone else. I realized in the midst of my fear of being imperfect that God had literally given me everything I needed to be effective for that appointed time. It wasn't what I wanted, but it was everything someone else needed. If I performed the way I envisioned, I would have been a useless being covered in vanity. I could have had a great voice and recited every line impeccably well and held the effectiveness of an empty ice tray.

When we shoot for the stars in an unfeasible universe of perfection, our level of transparency diminishes and our gift becomes impractical and inauthentic. Be intentional about being purposeful in your gift, because, when aiming for perfection, the target will never remain still.

Reflection:

- What areas of your life are you struggling to appear close to perfection?

- What are the dangers in trying to be perfect?

- Instead of trying to be perfect, how can you improve your perspective?

PETAL XVII
Sip & Serve

For the past few years, I have been fortunate to have Jodie Johnson as a beacon of light in my world. If there were a slot in Merriam Webster's Dictionary, her name would factor somewhere in between *astounding* and *phenomenal.* Production guru and entrepreneur extraordinaire, she somehow manages to find quality time in her ever-moving world for me. Every once in awhile, I have the privilege to be in her presence as she shares the ins and outs of her life. She discloses the good, the bad, and the ugly in an effort to guide me along my individual journey. What makes our time so special is that she allows me to strip down my emotional barriers in a nonjudgmental space. I never have to worry about our secrets ending up on the marquee of our church building or serve as material for her engagement. I can let go and be free from the pinball-machine-like thoughts bouncing around in my head. She is one of the greatest sources of relief in my world, and I couldn't be more eternally grateful for her presence and position in my life.

Another important figure in my world is my dear friend "Eva". Eva is a preschool teacher with hopes of owning multiple preschool centers. Along with teaching and singing, she loves encouraging and inspiring young women. Eva is one of the sweetest most sincere people I have ever encountered. Her poise, humility, character, and integrity are just a few reasons why I absolutely adore this young woman. Her aspirations consistently motivate her to be great in everything she plans to accomplish. Though as wonderful and remarkable as she is, it is sometimes difficult for Eva to see how amazing and essential she is to the world. She pinpoints her weaknesses before honing in on her strengths. She becomes discouraged by her mistakes rather than rejoicing in her victories. She could stare in a mirror and become blinded by one flaw while neglecting to see the countless, breathtaking traits staring back at her.

One of my goals in life is to counsel Eva the way Jodie has counseled me. Just as Jodie, I've aspired to live my life in a way that faithfully reminds Eva of the unique jewel in the crown of life she is. She inspires me everyday to be great and how to adhere to the principles Jodie is instilling in me. As my mentor pours into me, I desire to pour into Eva. The greatest and most pivotal attribute about this movement is as Eva gets older and truly enters into her purpose, she will have the assignment to pour into someone else.

Often times our focus shifts from ourselves to the issues around us. Our perspective, which was once clear, becomes hazy. The things that once made sense now seem unfamiliar. Yet through that haze, God orchestrates our lives to come in contact with people who have been where we are. Through supernatural confirmation, we in turn see their life mirror our own and, through a mutual trust, we discover how they made it over the hurdles we are coincidentally and concurrently facing. Our obligation becomes this: *Be a student in order to become a teacher.* We are required to submit to a designated authority figure in an effort to learn from their experience as we learn to formulate our own. Once these invaluable lessons are applied and implemented in our own lives, those priceless nuggets of greatness are given to those who are trailing behind us in similar shoes. Nana used to say, *"What makes you think your life is about you?"* If we fail to mentor someone else, we become emotional, selfish hoarders subconsciously stashing that wisdom within ourselves.

Robert "Bob" Montgomery Knight is more than a retired American basketball coach, but one of the most well-known and respected icons in the sports industry. Affectionately known as *The General*, Knight has won 902 NCAA Division I Men's College Basketball games. One of the most recognized players of his 1969-1974 United States Military Academy team is the phenomenal Mike "Coach K" Krzyzewski. After resigning from duty in 1974, Krzyzewski spent one year under Knight as an assistant coach with the Indiana Hoosiers. In 1980, Krzyzewski began his reign as the head coach of Duke University Men's Basketball Team. The lessons and teachings of Knight enabled Krzyzewski to surpass Knight with winning 903 NCAA Division I games. The relationship between Knight and Krzyzewski has blossomed into a realm of respect, dignity, and love. Krzyzewski never hesitates to pay homage to the man who not only developed his love for the game, but the role and responsibilities of an effective coach. In turn, Krzyzewski, using the same tactics he learned from Knight and a plethora of his own, created a coaching tree; a line of great men who have had the opportunity to learn from the great Coach K himself; one in particular is Johnny Dawkins. Seen by many as "next in line" to inherit the Duke throne, Dawkins was one of Krzyzewski's prized recruits in 1982-1986. Just like Krzyzewski, after his NBA career, Dawkins returned to Duke in 1998 as an assistant coach before accepting the head coach position at Stanford University in 2008. This totem pole of mentorship made it possible for all three remarkable men to hold a monumental place in sports history. Without their individual humility, willingness to learn, and preparation to teach, their success would have been deferred because of unnecessary arrogance and pride.

I am convinced the major components concerning the effectiveness of our individual journeys are based on two things: a pitcher and a cup. A pitcher receives whatever is desired with the intention to pour its contents into something else for another to receive. Interestingly enough, two things occur:

1. When the pitcher releases its contents, it must return to be refilled. This ensures the pitcher remains purposeful and submitted to a vital source.

2. The pitcher typically releases its contents into a cup or smaller vessel, meaning the entire contents of the pitcher cannot be emptied into the smaller vessel because the vessel can only consume what it can handle - a little at a time. The cup is only given more when what was previously given is sensibly consumed.

This movement is a never-ending circle of life. Therefore, with no movement, your journey and the journey of another are bound to perish. Ensure that somewhere in your life you are able to identify your pitcher and cup, because the contents given to and released from the pitcher are useless, pointless, and inoperable if stagnant.

Reflection:

- Who is your "pitcher"? What specific qualities do you admire about him/her?

- How often do you spend quality time with your mentor?

- What are three things your "pitcher" has instilled in your life?

- Who is your "cup"? Why do you desire to take this individual under your wing?

- How are you implementing the lessons learned from your "pitcher" into your designated "cup"?

PETAL XVIII
Riddle Me This

To Kenny with love…

Have you ever met someone that fascinated the quintessence of time? Someone who had a way of making every second of every minute of every hour pay attention to their presence? Someone whose character and integrity undeniably assisted with the positivity of any atmosphere? I have.

As a freshman trying to find her footing in college, Hamptonians who knew their identity and how to operate freely and unapologetically in their purpose captivated me. Whether President of the Student Government Association or top information systems technology student in the any graduating class, I was in awe of excellence, achievement, and fortitude. I guess it was those *"I wanna be just like _____ when I grow up"* moments that kept me focused and ambitious in school. The relationships I built with these extraordinary people have undoubtedly shaped my life. And even after they graduated and moved on into their careers, the incredible and incomparable history they left behind permeated my mind at the beginning of every new semester. I had major shoes to fill; one pair in particular, that of Dr. Kenneth Levar Riddle.

I don't remember the time or day we met. I don't remember what he wore or who was around. I don't remember the weather or the event that allowed our paths to cross. But I remember his smile and his laughter. I remember his energy. I remember his resilience and his determination to succeed. I remember his adoration for his mother and love for his fiancée. I remember his loyalty to his friends and family and his passion for the medical field of pharmacy. I remember those ginormous, big brother hugs and heart-to-heart talks about life. I remember his reprimand and *"Tam, you know better because you're better than that"* conversations. But most of all, I remember one of the most monumental attributes of his character…and I remembered it the day he fatally left this Earth.

In August 2005, Kenny died in an unexpected, tragic car accident that shook more than my world, but also the lives of every single person he knew, loved, and touched. Through the years of our friendship, I never once saw him conform to anything or anyone. Kenny defined originality. He lived his life from his heart and from the passion of his soul. He never needed to prove himself for the appeasement or approval of others because his life spoke for itself. Kenny made it a point to stand out, to be the one who went against the grain, and to become his own person. As I held his hand for the last time in his hospital room, it dawned on me that the world had just lost a treasure of a man because there would never be another Kenny Riddle. There is an array of great nuggets of wisdom I have learned from him, but the greatest of them all wasn't in anything he said, but how he lived.

Life is a *Catch 22*. We have the power to do whatever we choose with it, but have no control over its longevity. As precious as it is, we unconsciously take each moment for granted because subconsciously we know another one will come. But how unimaginable would it be to not only treasure the blessing of life, but to live that life with boldness and clarity for *you*? When we live our lives for the sanction of others, we lose sight of our worth and individuality. We become robots to the decadence of a fickle society and forfeit our ability to operate fully and effectively in our gifts. Life isn't daring when we follow the crowd. Instead, it becomes predictable, monotonous, and utterly boring. It is only when we create our own paths, our own rules, and our own standards that force the world to turn its ear to the beat of our own drum.

The legendary Robert Frost stated in his infamous poem "The Road Not Taken" that *"I took the [road] less traveled by, and that has made all the difference."* We can live our lives as basic followers, afraid of taking risks and fearful of the uncomfortable seasons that will inevitably rear its ugly head. Or, like our traveler, stand against the odds set before us, strategize ways to leap over difficult hurdles, and start the journey designed by us. Conformity may produce change, but it's only through our independence that individuality is bred. Examine the pavement of your roads, for the deserted ones that desire wear could be the greatest journey your life has ever seen.

Reflection:

- What are three things that make you different from everyone else?

- How are you applying your uniqueness to your personal dreams and goals?

- If nothing, what can you do differently to apply these things to your journey?

PETAL XIX
Tragedies in Target

First Lady Trina Jenkins partners with her husband in leading the disciple-developing movement of the First Baptist Church of Glenarden.

Princess Myers, blogger of Penelope Toop (Darling), specializes in exquisite party hats, decorative accessories, and extraordinary knick-knacks in an effort to make any space absolutely stunning.

Crystal Jackson works for the Department of Education while aspiring to become a school counselor in the Maryland Educational System.

Stephanie Young is the Associate Communications Director for The White House.

Designer and owner of Melanie Marie, New Yorker Melanie White specializes in authentic and stunning accessories and handbags.

Celebrity hairstylist LaNyce Oldham is the owner of The Funk Salon in Federal Hill, Baltimore, Maryland while serving as a motivational writer and speaker to young adults within the DMV area.

Precious Frazier, owner and founder of Nutritional InnerG, is a Natural Nutrition & Lifestyle Coach, encouraging men and woman to create practical health and fitness goals.

Yolanda Keels-Walker is an entrepreneur specializing in beauty, product development, and business coaching.

These and a host of others are women of purpose, destiny, and vision who, despite unfortunate moments of unforeseen setbacks, endured the race set before them....all while keeping their clothes on. In various ways, these women have influenced and impacted my life and, through provision and promise, continuously inspire me to become a better woman...all while keeping their clothes on. Their grind and work ethic is contagious, because they have proven the standard they've set for themselves is a lifestyle worth living for...all while keeping their clothes on. However, on a quick run to the heavenly establishment of Target, I quickly discovered that everyone doesn't esteem the same visionaries or reverence the same work ethics as I do of what it is considered to be a woman of noble character.

While perusing the Papyrus card section, I overheard a group of teenage girls reverencing the latest reality VH1 television show *Love & Hip Hop: Atlanta*. *Love & Hip Hop* tracks the lives of several African-American women and how they handle their working and romantic relationships in the "Dirty South". With a series of episodes aired, *Love & Hip Hop* has caused dramatic tension and controversy in the eyes of its viewers. While some clinch their pearls at the ignorant, classless, and demoralizing portrayal of some of these African-American women, others praise the "keeping it real" depiction and, like these young girls, admire to become these false pretenses of sophistication they see.

It breaks my heart to see women conform to the negative stereotypes already placed before them. In the era of slavery, full lips and voluptuous bodies made the black woman an object of sexual degradation and humiliation. Now, that once demeaning perception has become a voluntary and preferred way of life. I believe women are inheritably born with a strength to manage whatever comes their way. Whatever hurdles they encounter are accepted as being a part of their own race. Therefore, I am baffled by the lengths women will go through in order to be seen, heard, and relevant in this day in age. They will consciously sell their potential, intelligence, and competence for a dollar amount that will never equate to their self-worth. And when the currency inevitability increases, what can she give when she's already given her soul?

A former friend of mine, who once held the mind and merit of a universal scholar, sold herself to this classless and debasing industry. Plastered across the Internet are pictures and videos of her out-of-shape birthday suit and misappropriated belief of attraction and flair. With the infinite reach of the Internet, the world will forever attach her future ambitions with the decisions she's committed to today. Many, including myself, have made numerous attempts to rescue her from this lifestyle. Many have attempted to cover the root of this exposure with love, compassion, prayer, and help. What hurts even more is somewhere in America, the company she keeps encourages her behavior and has led her to believe that in order for her to transcend beyond her wildest dreams, she must renounce her value. She has the intelligence of a CEO, biomedical scientist, collegiate professor, or influential politician. Yet, instead of walking in her greatness, she's chosen a prodigal path with no hopes of returning home.

Here's my issue.

Somewhere between the playground and prom, the adolescent girls of this generation are lacking a plethora of women to admire and regard. Our children embrace television over books. They know every heroine on reality television but are not reading on or above their grade level. They can quote every hip-hop song but miss the importance of writing and speaking in a complete sentence. I'm not implying all television is detrimental to the development of our children. Yet, when I was coming up, Claire Huxtable proved that a woman could be a wife, mother and full-time lawyer. Whitley Gilbert opened the world to paintings, sculptures, and the life of an art historian.

Vivian Banks depicted the importance of family loyalty while raising her children in a home of humor and humility. There was a push for education and excellence in hopes of becoming originators of positive change and forward movement. *The sky is the limit* was the manifested mantra and desired execution. Yet, as the sun rises and sets today, women are more concerned with who's talking about them behind their back than walking in the confidence of knowing who they are themselves.

The time for saving our babies is now… literally. The current cynical days of bombarding our children's reason with unrealistic ideologies of success are disheartening, disturbing, and disgusting. Often times, people fill the air with their dreams and aspirations for our children without taking those things floating in the air and putting them into action. Remove the ceiling that's over our children that incites them to believe their highest potential involves vulgar language, too much make-up, and a fishnet skirt. Replace their iPods with novels. Enhance their culture beyond a magazine and give them the exposure of a museum. Set an example so your actions overpower your words, because sometimes their world is more impacted by the things they see you do rather than the things they hear you say. Women, regardless of class, color, or creed, you are queens; walk in your royalty.

Reflection:

- Who is someone you know falling by the wayside of integrity?

- How is their behavior detrimental to themselves and others?

- What are three ways you can intervene and help them discover their self-worth?

PETAL XX
Alone

One of the first games I learned how to play as a child was *Scrabble*. My parents procured the infamous game when my siblings and I were younger in an effort to enhance our personal vocabulary while in school. The concept behind their tactic was genius. We would play the game as a family and, when given the opportunity to play a word, we were forced to provide its definition. In the event we knew the word but not the correct definition, we not only had to look up the word, but points were deducted from our score. In order to prepare for these scholarly games, I would spend isolated time by myself to not only strategize tactics to use in the game, but also to learn new words on my own. These strategies and clever plays were only developed when I created ample time away from any distractions. Whether from people or things, I needed to be alone in order for my efforts to match my desire to win the game.

I think, just as *Scrabble*, life requires strategies. It demands that as we move throughout the board of life, we create arrangements to advance ourselves in the game. But the creation and the benefits of these strategies develop when we remove ourselves from the crowd and get alone.

There is an odd and negative connotation that comes with being alone. Think about it: sitting alone at a lunch table; sitting alone in a pew at church; sitting alone at a restaurant. Some of the first thoughts that stroll through the mind of an observer mirror, *"Wow, they sure are lonely,"* or *"I wouldn't want that to be me."* Our subconscious naturally leans to the end of the pity scale, feeling remotely sorry for the person that appears to be their only fan.

I disagree.

There is a vast difference between loneliness and solitude. Loneliness stems from brokenness. When something we've been connected to over a period of time unexpectedly parts ways, loneliness displays its unpleasant head. However, solitude illustrates tranquility. Solitude allows one to clear their mind from the tumbleweeds life blows their way. It's the ability to get alone and remain content in being there. It is in our solitude where silence gains its voice. Perspectives change, ambitions grow, and passions are generated through the exclusion of sound. Eliminating the presence of things that petition our attention is the most effective way to hone in on our inner peace and serenity.

Lord Byron once said, *"I only go out to gain a fresh appetite of solitude."* Spend time with the people you love and doing the things that bring you joy, but crave and create time making yourself a priority. Get alone; the world will be there when you get back.

Reflection:

- Are you having more moments of solitude or loneliness?

- In your opinion, what are the effects of a lonely spirit?

- What are the things you enjoy doing by yourself?

- How can you make more time doing things you love without feeling pressured to involve others?

PETAL XXI
Peas & Carrots

In 1994, the world was introduced to the celebrated character Forrest Gump. The self-entitled film illustrated the life of a naïve, low-IQ, Alabama native who falls in love with his best friend Jenny on his first day of school. Writer Winston Groom describes the relationship between Forrest and Jenny as a comparison of two vegetables that are commonly served together: peas and carrots. Although different, the "peas and carrots" bond is more than a clichéd expression; they add a noteworthy variety to any vegetable medley. Forrest and Jenny, though as different as these veggies, both needed each other for their own individual purposes. These two showed me that when it comes to friendships, I too need some peas and carrots in my interpersonal relationships. Through an extensive period of self-reflection, here are four types of relationships that should be held in your corner of friends.

The **ADVANCER** is the friend who strives to help you become your best *you*. They are typically the friend who has known you the longest and have watched you develop through the years. The bond you have is reciprocal; you are not just leeching from what they bring into your life, but you are pouring into them as well. The advancer literally assists in developing you into all that God has called you to be.

The **ARCHITECT** is your mentor. This individual helps you set reachable goals in order to fulfill your dreams. The architect is your biggest fan because they believe in you and your future. If you're a football player in the middle of a game, they are more than your sideline cheerleader. The architect will supply you with water for replenishment, a bench for rest, and a play when you are out of maneuvers. Your architect is preferably older and one who has been there and done that. They're knowledgeable insights, wise counsel, and sound judgment provide significant clarity as you face various tests and trials.

The AGGRAVATOR does exactly that – aggravate the hell out of you. You and your aggravator have a love/hate relationship. Your aggravator is strategically designed to challenge you in the areas of your life where you think you have it all together. They critique your every move and tell you all of the things you don't want to hear. One of the essential attributes of your aggravator is their ability to view your life from all of the angles you can't see. The key to receiving your aggravator's guidance is understanding that their advice is meant to help you, not hurt you. You will struggle, buttheads, and have numerous seasons of audacious conversations because you both are individually passionate about life. Yet, the greatest thing about your aggravator is that no matter what happens, they will always have your best interest at heart. Essentially, in order for you to grow, their tough love is necessary.

The ADVISOR is the friend that spiritually holds you accountable. This friend intercedes on your behalf when everyone else struggles to understand your situation. The advisor is concerned about your heart and soul. They enrich your life with gentle wisdom and provide significant counsel. Advisors help you stay on track as you progress toward your vision with a sincere and discerning voice of reason. The advisor serves as your accountability partner, stationed to put you back in line if you fall out of place. One of the fascinating attributes about the advisor is their willingness to stoop down in the muck to grab you out if necessary. They aren't pushy or aggressive, but incredibly understanding and patient, because your sanity and personal success is as important to them as it is to you.

Knowing the position of the people in your life is necessary and vitally important. Identifying these roles should fall into one basic category: assets, not liabilities. If you can't assign one of these roles to the closest individuals in your world, reconsider the company you keep. All four roles need to be actively present in your world in order to promote a lifetime of balance. In a group of four friends, you can't have three advancers and one architect. Where's the accountability? Where is the healthy friction? Check the ingredients in your personal recipe of friendships because too much of anything inevitably ruins the flavor.

Reflection:

- Assess your "Inner Circle". Using the four types of individuals mentioned above, place the people closest to you in their respective categories based on their role in your life.

- How do these people in your life help or hinder your character?

- What relationships do you need to alter, mend, or eliminate?

PETAL XXII
Shaky Pedestals

Before these essays developed into a book, *The Petals of Nora Rose* was a blog. In January of 2012, my passion for writing began to boil over. At the time, it dawned on me I hadn't written anything in months. Whether a poem or a journal entry, I hadn't had the urge to document anything I was thinking or feeling. I brushed it off and literally suppressed the things I heard from God and remembered from my grandmother. Yet as that year progressed, I received an intense and challenging word from Bishop T.D. Jakes. At a special Saturday service for leaders of your church and community, he said, *"This is the year of your gifting. You are sitting on your gift and suffocating your greatness. Get up."*

Needless to say…I got up.

Now here's the thing; I've always enjoyed writing and excelled in numerous opportunities to showcase my writing style. But for me to call it a *gift* was pushing the envelope. Yet, in the midst of this internal battle between what I enjoyed doing and what I was called to do, I decided to stop fighting, open a book, and started to write. As I wrote, I noticed there were specific ideas and illustrations God had used to teach me things. There were lessons I had learned *(and still learning)* about myself, my life, my decisions, and my interactions with people. Before I knew it, those thoughts became journal entries and those journal entries were complied into a website of encouragement and inspiration for anyone who just needed a boost to get them through uncomfortable seasons.

One of the most intense and difficult aspects of writing is sharing what you've purged. As exciting as it was to launch and add weekly insights to this personal site, I cried each time I posted something new. It's one thing to get everything that's bubbling in your heart out. To be honest with yourself about the things you've done and who you are takes a magnitude of courage. However, it is a completely different dynamic to publicly share your emotional transparency with something as massive and limitless as the Internet. It goes beyond changing your status, location, or hairstyle on your social network sites for something more priceless is at stake – your character. The website was incredibly successful and reached more people than I anticipated. The support from hundreds of people I didn't know motivated me to keep writing even though the process was painful. But in the midst of my excitement, I grew upset, disappointed, and heartbroken that some of the people closest to me were not supportive, involved, or moved by this new chapter in my life.

By nature, I'm a giver. Whether you want to campaign for a presidency or run a marathon, I'm your biggest fan. I believe in supporting the vision of my family and friends as long and as hard as I can. It has nothing to do with expecting anything in return or feeling as if I'm obligated out of family ties or friendships to be an advocate in your corner; it literally is embedded in who I am. Still, it's comforting to have those same people in *my* corner. It's comforting to know in sharing the innermost personal and private pieces of myself the people who I love with everything in me would be my cheerleaders in this new quest of self-discovery, but many of them were nowhere to be found.

To be completely honest, I was beyond annoyed. I was hurt. I grew tired of reaching out for support. I was exhausted; advertising and promoting myself to those I didn't think I had to sell myself to. I was mortified when my site was being discussed in various states and time zones and not amongst the people who I spent time with every day.

At times, when it was discussed, some brushed it off. Some laughed. Some suggested I find something else to do because other things were more important to pursue than a career in writing. Resentment and bitterness began to take root as I witnessed my project and what I knew God placed on heart disregarded and ultimately ignored.

Then it dawned on me. People weren't upsetting me…I was upsetting myself. Expectation is a noose we inevitably hang ourselves with. Our thoughts will take a rope, make a collar knot, and place itself around our neck in an effort to end our frustration and anger. Expectation will create various realms of assumptions, generating images in our head of how things "should" pan out. However, these expectations and assumptions destroy our confidence and self-assurance. We should never become dependent on people to validate our gifts. Our gifts are God-given assets to the person He's designed us to become. When we expect people to be as passionate about our gifts as we are, we indirectly make their opinions more important than the assignment God has ordained for us. The validation of man cannot take precedence over the things God has called us do.

Don't get me wrong; there is nothing wrong with desiring support and reassurance from your closet confidants. You and the gifts you offer to the world are important, instrumental, and influential. There is only one of you, so don't take lightly your place in the world. Yet, if you don't receive that desired support and reassurance, don't dim the fire growing inside of you; it's a reason why it's there. God is bigger than the things and people who are around us. Often times, He will place us in certain circumstances to see whom we'll run to when our confidence meter is running low. Our expectation and hope should be placed in Him, the One who will never let us down or fail to acknowledge the promise instilled in us, primarily because He placed it there.

Remind yourself that people are human. Instead of being judgmentally savvy or growing discouraged when you feel overlooked, keep in mind that pedestals of perfection are intangible. Never remove the imperfection notch from someone's belt; it's a part of all of us. Instead, tap into the greatness you know you possess and pull out the strength to fight your fear with faith. Writer Richard Bach said, *"In order to win, you must expect to win."* If your aspiration is to be great, expect greatness. Believe and affirm your brilliance, so those who are to feed off of the fruit you bear will witness your confidence in an effort to find their own.

Reflection:

- Describe your support system and how they encourage you.

- Is their support important to you? Why or why not?

- How do you empower yourself? If you're not, what are three ways you can begin restoring your confidence?

PETAL XXIII
Tightropes

Weighing in at nearly 14,500 lbs. and reaching a high of 187 ft. lies the infamous, world-renowned *Torre Pendente di Pisa*, affectionately known as The Leaning Tower of Pisa. The tilted-tower is a *campanile*, or self-supporting bell tower and serves as the main tourist attraction in the quaint town of Pisa, Italy. This massive pillar of history is said to be one of the most breathtaking creations of any generation. However, no matter how captivating its being remains, it will forever be known for its imbalanced structure.

The origin of its tilt began during the tower's early stages of construction. The result of a poor foundation and ground too soft on one side to adequately support the building's weight, the tilt gradually increased before the tower was fully completed in the early 21st century. For decades, numerous architects, engineers, even spectators have pitched endless suggestions on how to straighten the Tower of Pisa, eliminating its lean altogether. Ironically, those suggestions were retaliated with two major rebuttals: 1) straightening the pillar would essentially lose the notoriety of the tower's centurial lean, and 2) many would rather the tower to topple and tumble over before an effort of perfection is attempted, let alone entertained. Though the completion of the tower contradicts its original blueprint, the world has praised its deformity. Instead of the tower being rectified or amended to align itself to its intended design, society not only labeled the tower based on its defect, but also desires to keep the tower in its deficient state.

Isn't it utterly amazing how the world does the same thing to us? We become known for our shortcomings, imperfections, and flaws. Our blots and blemishes become the bait of social ridicule. Unconsciously, people associate our identity with our insecurities, leaving us to feel as if our destiny is doomed for failure. In addition, even when we desire to use our respective "lean" for something greater, those around us condemn our efforts in fear of how our wholeness will affect their livelihood.

Allow me to introduce *The Tightrope Theory.*

Often times, we are challenged with balancing our sanity with our purpose. The question of how to manage *this* with *that* arises. It's as if we are constantly trying to hold up the world's expectations of us, as well as our own all the while trying to discover our identity. In short, society will throw us a tensioned wire and expect a tightrope circus segment leaving our lives to look like this:

While we're taught to desire this:

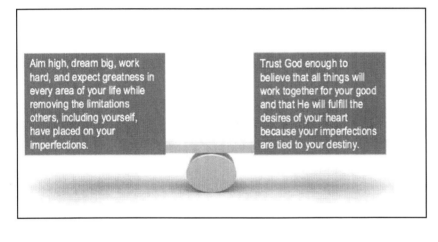

One of my favorite motivational speakers in the world is the incomparable Nick Vujicic. Hilarious, inspiring, and extraordinary are just a few ways to classify this internationally recognized man of God. He has traveled the world, transformed lives, and encouraged people from all walks of life to recognize their strategically designed purpose without arms and legs…literally.

When I first laid my eyes on Nick, my heart sunk beneath the soles of my platform heels. I was speechless. I never knew a human being could successfully let alone physically exist without limbs. I remember feeling overwhelmed with sadness, compassion, and an insurmountable amount of questions, theories, and prayers. Yet, when he spoke, I witnessed a young man who had more confidence then a walking, arm-swinging, fully limbed human being. His physical appearance came as a surprise to his parents who, when heard the condition of their son, battled with what to do next. Yet, through complete surrender, his parents heeded to the voice of God, remained still, and gained comfort in knowing that this intentional blueprint for Nick's life was designed for something greater.

From periods of depression to suicidal attempts, Nick shares his limbless experience with such passion and purpose. The fear of being infinitely taunted, teased and tormented made his thought life indescribably difficult to bear. Yet, with an act of boldness, Nick embraced and owned his individuality. He learned how to perceive his uniqueness through the eyes of God and not that of man. When he redirected his attention from what he couldn't control to Whom is in control, his outlook changed. He became fascinated with how God was still able to use someone whom the world had already written off.

It is literally impossible to count the number of people who have been, and continue to be, blessed by Nick's testimony. Destinies fulfilled and inner peace gained all because Nick chose to use his "lean" for something impactful rather than shameful. At any time, he could have ended his life. He could have become a recluse and hid himself from the limelight. He could have grown infinitely angry with God for creating him this way or even spent his entire life praying that his situation would change. Instead, he stopped praying that his circumstance would change but that others would be changed through his circumstance. His "lean", in time, gave him liberty.

You are the landlord of your lean. You own it. It will forever be attached to you because the Creator thought enough of you to bless you with it. Regardless of what the world thinks of your lean or how they hope to change it, it was never meant to conform, but to assist in the beautification process of your destiny. Your "lean" may not be pretty. It probably isn't popular or welcoming. Yet, when your attention shifts from feelings to fulfillment, you begin to see things differently.

The incomparable John K. Jenkins, Sr. pastors the First Baptist Church of Glenarden in Upper Marlboro, MD. I could never successfully put into words the magnitude of how his wisdom, leadership, reason, and teachings have colored my world. His guidance and support have impacted my life since I was a child and throughout my adulthood. There are so many profound lessons I've learned from him, but the one that changed my life focused on my psyche. Pastor stated ever so simply one Sunday morning that, *"How we think is how we live because what we think drives our behavior."* Become more cognizant of the thoughts you have toward yourself… flaws and all. Spend time deciphering those not-so-appealing entities and adjust your thinking, recognizing the possibility of beauty that resides there; trust me…it's there.

Reflection:

- What do you consider to be your "lean"? How does your lean make you feel?

- What opportunities or ambitions have you put on hold because of your lean?

- How can you adjust your thinking and use your lean to better yourself? Someone else?

PETAL XXIV
Trick Bags: Shaken, Not Stirred

Recently, I went on by far the worst blind date of my entire life. There was a point in the evening when I secretly hoped E.T. would return to Earth in search of Elliott to see if he saw a sequel in their near future. I dozed off twice, almost died from an allergic reaction, and ran into an old flame that looked better than Black Friday sales.

One of the most nerve-wrecking elements to being the single friend in your circle of wedded pals is your married friends, more than often, want to set you up with their other eligible friends. It's as if there's an annual marriage convention in some secluded corner of the universe and in order to renew your membership each year you have to match-make two of your single friends together. Never mind the inevitable pressure you put on these two singles; for in the event their potential union fails, everyone is left feeling noticeably awkward and highly uncomfortable.

Naturally, these two singles will share something in common (i.e. sports teams, birthdays, music genres, etc.). The married couple then shares with each other how, based on this similarity, Single Friend 1 and Single Friend 2 would be perfect for each other. Then, after they pat each other on the back for this "ah ha" moment of brilliance, the matchmakers take that commonality, mix it with the perfect meet-up, throw in the gassed-up versions of each friend, shake it up in a trick bag of hope, and **BAM**...out pops a meaningful, legitimate, and authentic relationship. Absolutely not.

Nothing about me screams, *"Please, set me up with your friend"*. I'm abnormally chill when it comes to dating, let alone being "hooked up". It is not an arrogant mode of operation; it's just a preference. I sincerely enjoy organically meeting someone new and seeing what happens in its own strength. Something about happenchance intrigues me, while, on the flip side, being set-up annoys my livelihood. The set-up saturates the meet-up and any date thereafter in unconscious expectation. Both parties feel obligated to make something work even if there is nothing there. So when I first met "Tim" and we weren't making conversation let alone a love connection, I was immediately reminded how the aspired antics of my married friends don't work for Tam Sease.

The illustrated pitch of Tim was Picasso-inspired. "The Johnsons", my newly married friends, sat me down in their renovated sunroom and talked my head off about their bachelor friend Tim, a chemical engineer from Chicago, Illinois. They gassed this man up enough to drive from here to Utah and back …with two rest stops. Tim recently moved to DC a few months ago and was looking for *Mrs. Right*. Not too sure why The Johnson pair thought this desired woman and I shared the same identity, but nevertheless, I threw on my "good sport" hat and agreed to dinner at a quaint and charming restaurant in Chinatown. Now something said, *Tam, you should probably have a clutch move in your back pocket; alert a friend that the 'bail me out of this disaster' call may occur tonight.* Against my better judgment, I ignored that faint voice, played fair, and endured the most strenuous two hours of my life.

If he wasn't talking about his mother the entire night, he was reciting the lyrics to his favorite N'Sync songs. If he wasn't scratching his armpits (because apparently the new deodorant he was trying out this week was causing some sort of inflamed reaction that the entire restaurant needed to know about) he was insulting my skin tone; apparently I wasn't light enough for his liking. After discovering his atheistic views towards my faith and his intense interest in our maître d', it was clear that the only commonality Tim and I shared were the initials in our first names. Needless to say, my married friends are still on punishment and indefinitely suspended from all activity from their fluke dating services.

When I turned 29, I remember feeling inadequate and unfulfilled when it came to relationships. I became obsessed with all I had failed to accomplish on my journey rather than the invaluable lessons learned along the way. Time was moving at lighting speed and I, husbandless and childless, was failing trying to keep up with the crowd. Every weekend was either a baby shower or a wedding. I remember shopping at Target so much in a particular month, a sales associate finally asked, *"When is your time coming?"* The third wheel role was getting old and desperation started kicking in and I grew fearful of entering another age bracket still single. However when I turned 30, I embraced my singleness like never before. Something about everything was different. I felt smarter, wiser, sexier, and more driven in this new decade than ever before. Yet, even in this new season of contentment, it seemed unrealistic to some people in my life to be both single and happy. How could I possibly be single and whole in the space of time? Conversations went from *"How are you,"* to *"Are your eggs still working"*. It became a monthly mission for certain friends of mine to connect me with someone….anyone. However, I find it impeccably insulting to be a project or case file in the eyes of some of my married friends simply because I'm, what appears to be, one of the last single girls. Now let's be clear: I desire a relationship, marriage, and children and at times I do feel the inevitable marital-maternal itch…but bless the Lord for Cortisone – I'm just not ready. Yet, the pressure they've placed in making me someone's counterpart has hurt more than anything because though my desires may be one thing, I'm perfectly sane in my current posture without one or the other.

Anthony "Tony" Adams, affectionately known as my *Ace of Spade*, is not only one of my best friends in the universe, but he is my brother from another mother. I met Tony my freshman year of college through his older brother Tommy, a senior star-athlete from Woodbridge, Virginia. On the night of Tommy's senior basketball game, he not only introduced me to his kid brother, but also made me promise that I would keep an eye on him next year, for Tony would attend Hampton in the fall. Tommy kept a close eye on me my freshman year. He ensured that I stayed out of trouble and remained faithfully cautious of the company I kept. So it was only right that I returned the favor and did the same for his younger sibling. Yet, who would have thought that Tony and I would become inseparable confidants throughout undergrad and our adulthood? To this day, Tony and I are thick as thieves, always ready to take over the world.

There are an infinite amount of things I adore about my good friend Tony, but my all time favorite attribute is his ability to shut out peer pressure before it's even spoken. Through the years, he has development firm discernment when it comes to personal areas of his life. When someone attempts to include him in their picture of how they think *his* life should be, he blatantly makes it clear that his life is his own and unsolicited advice isn't needed, warranted, or required. He remains comfortable in his skin, proving that his world doesn't need to emulate those around him in order to feel complete. Everyone he builds relationships with respect and understand that when his time arrives, it will appear in God's time and not a moment earlier.

Too often, when one's singleness is brought into the limelight, it is followed by a weird and negative connotation of incompleteness. It's absurd to believe that in order for a single's world to function properly they have to be romantically involved with another. It's even more ludicrous for that same single to settle being with anybody just to avoid being with nobody. Is it really *that* unreasonable to cultivate yourself first – your interests, your passions, your goals, your identity – and *then* watch love reveal itself in due time? *Difficult?* Yes. *Challenging?* Indeed. *Impossible?* I think not.

For the "Pressure People", chill… in real life. Pressure from those closest to us can either challenge our progression or handicap our ambition. Think first and tread lightly. Though your intentions may serve in the right place, your actions may sing another tune. We appreciate your hearts and your desires to see us successful, blissful, fulfilled, and one with ourselves. Just remember this simple fact – there's a great possibility we are already those things and more. And for the defendants in a courtroom of pressure, stop defending yourselves and allow your life to speak for itself. Make yourself a priority and focus on fulfilling your assigned purpose, not the picturesque imitations designed by friends and family. Become immune to settling for anything or anyone and create an adventurous life for yourself; your peace of mind will thank you for it.

Reflection:

- Are you the culprit of unsolicited peer pressure with your loved ones?

- How can your pressure challenge their progression?

- How can your advice handicap their ambitions?

- How do you know when it is best to stay in your lane and allow your loved ones experience life for themselves?

PETAL XXV
Elsewhere

Dear Future Tam,

I had an interesting moment thinking of you today. As I drove home on a midday summer afternoon, I began to think of what you would be like. Whether you would loc your hair or grow out your perm. If you would buy that new car you've been eying or ride your current wheels until the good Lord takes it on home to glory. If you would quit your job and move across the world to create a new life for yourself. Thoughts, and more thoughts, and more thoughts of you...the future you.

I began to picture your life ten years from now...and then five years from now...until finally I began to think about tomorrow. "What will you do with your tomorrow", I asked. Would you still be in debt? Would you still be overweight? Would publishing this book ever end? Would you still watch others live their life without claiming your own? Tears decided to join the thinking-party, not only blurring my eyesight but also ultimately forcing me to pull the car over and unleash a heavy heart on the side on Interstate 495.

I cried for everything I had, everything I didn't, and everything I longed for. I cried for my lack of peace and nonexistent serenity. I cried for my poor decisions and their life-long consequences. I cried for us. It was if the enemy GPS'd my location and met me there with all of the things that held me bound. I couldn't fight for myself. I couldn't encourage myself. So I just cried. And as I began to catch my breath and pull myself together, an 18-wheeler passed by with a slogan that silenced the noise in and outside of our head: **Gather, Plant, and Grow...Somewhere Else.**

As I sat there in what appeared to be spirit-led silence, I noticed that all along I had been parked near a dead field. What was once an opened pasture full of life was now a deserted and abandoned territory covered in weeds and damaged soil. Ironically, in the midst of this lifeless terrain posted a phone number of the company for anyone interested in planting their crops on this property. Now who in their right mind would do business with this company, let alone invest in a dying environment and expect an exceptional return was ludicrous to me in that moment. This particular business must employ and network with a group of incompetent people that believe this marketing plan would heighten their notoriety and increase profit sales.

It's funny how God speaks to us, Tam. We think we've stumbled across something odd or simplistic, but He purposefully shows His face in a way that only you and I understand. In that moment, He revealed something so powerful. Between that 18-wheeler and this horrific former grassland was the fire under our feet I needed. Tam, you can't stay here, baby girl. Gather yourself, plant your feet, and prepare to grow...somewhere else.

It's clear and uncomfortably evident that you're dying. Granted, there are so many things aligning itself in your favor and an array of things that deserve your gratefulness. However, there are so many passions and desires burning inside of you that are gasping for air. You've spent so much time investing in things and people, and as a result, suffocated your talents and negated your purpose.

As amazing as it can be, life has a way of manipulating our vision. We will reach a particular pinnacle in our progression and, for a moment, believe "we've made it". Without warning, an invitation to the "Comfort Zone" will arrive and before we know it, we've grown complacent in in our efforts of personal development. The danger of complacency is that as our actions stay the same, our expectation grows. We begin to desire a better life for ourselves, but do nothing to achieve it. Society states we develop a gift of gab; talking a good game without putting in the work to achieve success. We become more consumed with the accumulation of accomplishments rather than the act of achievement. Like that dying pasture on 495, we won't tend our fields, water our roots, or plant ourselves in the core of our calling, but will invest in death and still expect something to grow.

Tam, I implore you to see yourself for who you are, Who's you are, and dust your anxiety off. You can't erase what you've done or dwell on what you haven't accomplished either. You can't worry about tomorrow, because as you know it will worry about it itself. If you're not seizing the moment placed in front of you, stop stressing over the things you haven't worked to achieve. Emotional entrapment places restraints on a colossal God who has the power to bring to pass the yearnings of your heart. Reflections should provide constructive criticism, but are ultimately meant to propel you to the next point on your journey. Take those passions and assignments God has called you to fulfill and move away from this death trap. Trust Him to do it, but plant yourself in an atmosphere that breeds life; it is only these places where growth can occur.

You should know that once I breathed and gathered myself, I moved from that dead place and made my way down that highway in effort to grow. Yet, my newly found motivation was based on doing the legwork first. I have a feeling that you will appreciate this effort. I'm confident in knowing that in due time, if I remain diligent and focused on Him, you will witness the bloom of deeply rooted flowers in a field of faithfulness, not fear.

See you soon.

Tam

Reflection:

- Are you planted in an environment where every area of your life can grow?

- If not, what steps can you take to relocate and plant yourself somewhere else? If yes, how is your return benefitting others?

- How are you making your future-self proud of the man/woman you will ultimately become?

About The Author

Tamra Sease is an English Educator and Blended Online Learning Coordinator for Prince George's County Maryland. Following the career paths of her grandparents, Tamra strives to design her craft of teaching to impact the lives of children through emphasizing the importance of higher education and perseverance through times of adversity. Her unique and versatile teaching methods motivate her students to reach beyond the limitations placed before them in an effort to excel in and outside of the classroom. She operates her professional career under the infamous quote, *"Every child, regardless of the disguise, knows what he or she is not. We must teach each child what he or she can become."*

Tamra is a writer and assistant director for The Press Play Company, LLC., specializing in theater and film production. A graduate of Hampton University, Tamra is also the proud daughter of Dr. & Mrs. Tillman R. Sease, Jr. and eldest sibling of Jacqueline Octavia and Brandon Tillman of Bowie, MD.

Visit tamrasease.com for additional resources and contact information.

Made in the USA
Middletown, DE
24 August 2015